D0293653

K
'9.95

"Important"

"An important book that must be read by all of us who want every possible advantage in these tricky times."

Martin Edelston
President
Boardroom Reports

"Insightful"

"Andrew Garvin has written an insightful guide on how excutives can gain a competitive edge by asking the right questions and finding the right answer. I hope that my competitors *don't* see this book."

Larry J. Kirshbaum
President/Chief Executive Officer
Warner Books, Inc.

"Powerful"

"*The Art of Being Well Informed* is a valuable book that will be received as a seminal work on the nature of information. Garvin sends a powerful, timeless message to all business. Information is no longer a luxury, but a necessity in today's marketplace. It is one of those few books that you'll keep on your desk rather than in your bookcase."

Frank Sonnenberg
President
RMI Marketing & Advertising
Author of Marketing to Win *and* Managing With a Conscience

"Clearly Put"

**"The thinking discipline clearly put forth in this book
has helped our company get a six million dollar problem
under control."**

William Stein Steinberg
President
Tradewell Inc.

"Invaluable"

**"This book is an invaluable resource for any executive
who makes decisions. Read it and keep it as a reference.
It will greatly increase your odds
for success in today's highly competitive environment."**

Frederick H. Fruitman
Managing Director
Loeb Partners Corporation

"Informative"

**"Truly informative....Mr. Garvin gets to the heart of the matter:
how business people can apply knowledge to their individual
business needs. This is truly a "hands on" book,
about how to get information—with names, addresses,
and phone numbers there for the taking."**

Donald R. Kornblet
President
Business Response, Inc.

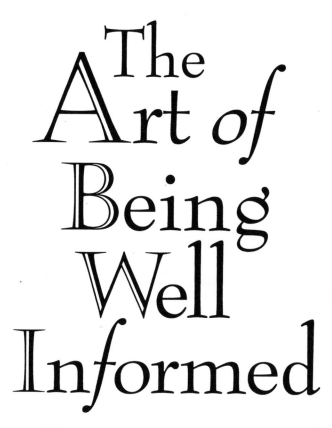

The Art of Being Well Informed

WHAT YOU NEED TO KNOW TO GAIN THE WINNING EDGE IN BUSINESS

Andrew P. Garvin

WITH ROBERT BERKMAN AND HUBERT BERMONT

AVERY PUBLISHING GROUP INC.
Garden City Park, New York

Cover Designer: Ann Vestal
Editors: Vanessa Elder and Elaine Will Sparber
Typesetter: Bonnie Freid
Indexer: Mary F. Tomaselli
Printer: Paragon Press, Honesdale, PA

Library of Congress Cataloging-in-Publication Data

Garvin, Andrew P.
    The art of being well informed: what you need to know to gain
the winning edge in business / Andrew P. Garvin with Hubert
Bermont, Robert Berkman.
    p. cm.
    Includes bibliographical references and index.
    ISBN 0-89529-576-8

    1. Communication in management. 2. Industry–United States–
Information services. 3. Information services–Guidebooks. 4.
Data bases–Guidebooks. I. Bermont, Hubert Ingram. II. Berkman,
Robert I. III. Title.

HF5718.G37 1993   658.4'5
                                                  QB193-20090

Copyright © 1993 by FIND/SVP, Inc.

All rights reserved. No part of this publication may be reproduced,
stored in a retrieval system, or transmitted, in any form or by any
means, electronic, mechanical, photocopying, recording or otherwise, without prior written permission of the copyright owner.

Printed in the United States of America

10 9 8 7 6 5 4 3 2

Contents

To Kira and Linda.

CREDITS

Grateful acknowledgment is made for permission to reprint:

Excerpt from *The Buffalo News*. Copyright Janice Okun, *The Buffalo News*. Reprinted by permission.

Excerpt from *American Business Directory* database. Copyright American Business Information. Reprinted by permission.

Excerpt from *SEC Online* database. Copyright 1984–1992 SEC Online, Inc. All rights reserved. Reprinted by permission.

Excerpt from *The Rochester Business Journal*. Copyright *The Rochester Business Journal*. Reprinted by permission.

Excerpt from *Predicasts PROMT* database. Copyright Predicasts. Reprinted by permission.

Excerpt from *Findex* database. Copyright Cambridge Information Group, Inc. Cambridge Information Group owns all rights in the information contained in the *Findex* database. Reprinted by permission.

Excerpt from *MAX* database. Copyright Claritas/NPDC. Reprinted by permission.

Excerpt from *Trade and Industry Index*. Copyright Information Access Company. Reprinted by permission.

Excerpt from *Business International* database. Copyright Business International. Reprinted by permission.

Excerpt from *Tradeline* database. Copyright IDD Information Services. Reprinted by permission.

Excerpt from *Disclosure Database*. Data provided by the *Disclosure Database*, Disclosure Inc., copyright 1992.

Acknowledgments

I wish to express my sincere thanks to all the dedicated professional people who have worked for and with me in the knowledge business throughout the past twenty years. Without them, this book would not have been possible. In particular, special contributions were made by Kathleen Bingham, Anne Dennis, Elke Kastner, Neal McIlvane, Tom Miller, and Frances Spigai.

Hubert Bermont and Robert Berkman provided much of the inspiration and the behind-the-scenes effort that helped make my concepts readable.

My thanks, also, to the staff of FIND/SVP and to the many individuals who provided comments and suggestions to help make this revised edition as up-to-date as possible.

—Andrew P. Garvin

Preface

Some years ago, a friend of mine called me in a panic. He was desperate. "My ten-week-old daughter has just been diagnosed with an apparently rare disease I can't even pronounce," he said. "She may die. The pediatrician has never even encountered a case before."

"How can I help?" I asked.

"I need to find out about this condition . . . I must find the best care . . . I must save her life!" he yelled.

Fortunately, since 1969 I've headed FIND/SVP, a company that helps business people find out what they need to know. I applied the same principles used in my business to help my friend.

After getting the correct spelling of his daughter's condition—"sub-glottic hemangioma"—we discovered in various medical textbooks, like the *Merck Manual* and *Current Therapy*, that it was very rare, especially in children so young.

"Now what?" my friend asked. "I want the greatest expert in the field to treat her!"

After I calmed him down, we proceeded with a step-by-step investigation. First, I suggested we find out as much as we could about the condition by reading everything that's been published about it. Some of the consultants and researchers at FIND/SVP helped by searching computer databases like *Health*

Periodicals Database and *Medline*. Others suggested the database offered by the National Organization for Rare Disorders. Through these, we found references to articles about the disease and treatment all the way back to 1966. We obtained the articles using a variety of firms that specialize in obtaining hard-to-find articles from medical journals and the like.

Within a day, my friend was a lay-expert on sub-glottic hemangiomas in children. By poring over the articles carefully, he unearthed names of doctors who specialize in this field. Four names kept coming up—two in the United States, one in Canada, and one in London. My friend called all of them and, armed with plenty of knowledge from his reading, was able to intelligently interview them. Finally, he picked one in Cincinnati. He flew his daughter there on a special medical plane, and an operation was quickly performed.

Happily, the little girl's life was saved.

I tell this story because it demonstrates how important it is to know how to become well informed. Sometimes it truly is a matter of life and death.

Most of the time, however, being well informed simply helps us to succeed at things we must do every day: solve problems, make business decisions, and explore opportunities.

Being well informed means having the right information and knowledge at the right time (and at the right price). The need to know—and to know quickly—is a key factor dominating our business and personal lives. Never before in history has there been so much information so readily available, but most of us have so little time to find it. We're too busy. Decisions have to be made *too* quickly. Just think about how the fax machine has sped up the pace of business in only a few years.

To compete effectively, we need to be continuously informed. Yet it always amazes me to see how few of my friends and business acquaintances really know how to find information—how to get smart fast about a new subject—or even how to ask the right questions in order to get the right answers.

Actually, it shouldn't be surprising, since finding information is not really taught in school or in college. Where do you learn that asking someone, "Do you have any information on . . ." is not nearly as effective as asking, "Who is the best person to ask for information on . . ."?

The purpose of this book is to help you ask better questions so you get better answers, and to acquaint you with all the aspects of today's information environment so you can benefit from it. Chapter 1 describes why it has become increasingly vital to be well informed, and why information is the key to success. Chapter 2 explains why it is so dangerous to make assumptions, and looks at the need for solid and reliable data. In Chapter 3, you'll learn how to formulate good questions— questions that will get you the answers you need to efficiently solve your business problems. Chapter 4 delineates the actual costs of the different types of information, and explains how you can determine what a particular piece of information is worth to you. Chapter 5 explains how to judge the quality of the information you get, and outlines the pitfalls of various information sources. In Chapter 6, you'll find a detailed examination of our information environment, including a look at new and future resources. Chapter 7 describes the world of online databases, and provides examples of database searches. "Information paralysis" is an all-too-common problem in today's world. Chapter 8 examines this peculiar disease, and discusses how it can be cured. Chapter 9 describes how to create your own information-gathering system, including a personal library and the use of information-gathering services. Finally, Chapter 10 provides a step-by-step guide to assembling an information report. Comprehensive listings of information sources, databases, information-gathering companies, and how-to books can be found in the appendices.

Knowing how to be well informed is something of an art. I hope you'll learn a little of it from this book.

Andrew P. Garvin
President
FIND/SVP, Inc.
New York

Introduction

The most important thing for business and professional people to have is often the most difficult thing for them to find: information. Information can make the difference between a decision and a guess, between success and failure, between wealth and poverty.

As the saying goes, knowledge is power. The ability to make successful decisions depends directly upon the amount of knowledge you have. Knowledge results from information. How you can become the kind of individual who can acquire valuable information quickly, easily, and economically is the subject of this book.

Books are published in spates. When a subject is "hot," a number of publishers jump into the fray with pertinent titles, but all the books tend to say the same thing. The subject of information is indeed one of the hottest. However, we have no intention of repeating what the others are saying. There are many fine books available that will tell you all about hundreds and hundreds of valuable sources of information. Among the most notable of these is Lorna Daniells' *Business Information Sources* (University of California Press, 1985) as well as others published more recently such as *The Business Information Desk Reference* (Macmillan, 1992). This is no such source book, although we do mention and list a number of the best sources in the text and in the appendices.

There are also many how-to books out there that explain, usually in technical terms, how to perform market research. These will tell you about the different kinds of research, about designing surveys and performing tabulations, and about a great variety of techniques that the average executive doesn't want to be bothered with. Some of the best of these how-to books are listed in Appendix VI. Our book is not a how-to book either, although we will try to tell you something about how to be an effective information-gatherer.

This book deals specifically with raising your "information consciousness." Until this consciousness is enhanced, all the source books and how-to books in the world will be of little value to you.

Raising your information consciousness means learning how to think in ways that result in your being well informed, in being infinitely more resourceful than you are now. This is not easy, but it is far easier than solving problems in, say, nuclear physics.

Being well informed takes time, effort, curiosity, and some thought. You have to be able to ask the right questions and to understand how the right answers may be found. If you can find the right information, you can use it. Clearly, the more you know about something, the better you can control your own situation. Knowledge is a synthesis of information. And knowing means winning.

Many people have no idea how to find what they need to know. This surprised us when we first researched this book in the early 1980s, and it is absolutely astonishing to us that this is still true today. The majority of executives and professionals often don't realize when they need information, whether or not it can be obtained, or how valuable it can be to them.

The evidence of this is everywhere. Ask a group of executives if they could briefly explain the information contained in such basic sources as the *Statistical Abstract of the United States,* or the *Thomas Register,* or the *Business Periodicals Index,* or the

Encyclopedia of Associations. We'll wager that few in the group can answer correctly. Knowledge is equally lacking in the ability to find and use the burgeoning number of online business sources as well. These are the "databases" of information available on your computer at the touch of a few keys. (If you are one of the people to whom the above basic sources are unfamiliar, don't worry. The purpose of this book is to raise your consciousness so that you'll *want* to be familiar with them, and *will* be familiar with them.)

The suffering caused by inadequate information-gathering is immeasurable. And it is responsible for nearly every professional, business, and even personal failure.

Many of these failures are big and complex. The Edsel is a classic example. But others can be perceived in everyone's day-to-day activities. Think back on your own experiences and on those of people you know. How many times have you erred or made a poor decision because you didn't have a key piece of information in advance? You overpaid for goods and services because you didn't know they were available cheaper elsewhere. You wasted hours standing in the wrong line. You tried in vain to obtain something from a government bureaucracy, armed with the wrong papers. You went on vacation and ended up in a dismal, miserable place.

Paradoxically, while most people have little awareness of information's vital role in their lives, they often simultaneously suffer from a feeling of "information overload," or, in the words of author Saul Wurman, "information anxiety." Many of us feel swamped by the magazine articles, reports, memos, and other pieces of information piling up on our desks. While it may seem that the problem is too much information, in reality the problem still comes down to a lack of "information savvy"—the ability to identify the most useful information and manage it in an organized and focused manner. The cure for those suffering from information overload is the same as it is for those who have little awareness about the availability of information: increasing information consciousness. The information-conscious executive knows not only why information is important and where to find it, but how to selectively obtain the most useful and relevant information and how to put it to work efficiently.

On the bright side, since we last updated this book in 1985, a number of enlightened companies have begun to see the strategic importance of information, and the need to set up an organized and disciplined system for capturing, analyzing, and utilizing data. One of the fastest growing new disciplines during the last few years is a field called "competitive intelligence." Persons in this area analyze competitors and competitive conditions and funnel that data into their companies' strategic planning, marketing, and research and development operations. The way these professionals accomplish their mission is by finding and analyzing *information*. There's even a professional organization devoted to this discipline: the Society of Competitive Intelligence Professionals, or SCIP.

Who are these people and companies that are now information conscious? We would undoubtedly find that people with a high level of information consciousness have the following characteristics:

- They tend to read a lot.
- They keep lots of files on all kinds of things.
- They have an insatiable curiosity.
- They prefer an authoritative opinion to gossip.
- They can quickly translate problems into information questions.

In short, these people enjoy a high degree of information literacy. We all know about and have been exposed to Intelligence Quotients all of our lives. But these people have developed a very high Information Quotient. There is, of course, no such thing as an Information Quotient test yet, because no one has developed one. Perhaps someday we will.

We'd like to end this introduction with a brief but very significant little story. A few years ago, we were at a popular seaside resort where a few motels competed for the local tourist business. In booking a room in one of the motels, we by chance discovered that the owner had absolutely no idea what rates were being charged by his competitor located less than half a mile away! It was not surprising to learn some months later that the owner's motel had been taken over by a chain. He had lost his business.

This book is not written solely for the executive in a big corporation. It is written for all executives everywhere, and for professionals, scientists, consultants, technicians, and, yes, even motel owners. While our emphasis will be on business and professions, the lessons of this book apply to all of life, for if you cannot use information to create business successes, then it is doubtful you can use information for personal achievement.

In *The Paper Chase*, which deals with the rigors and vicissitudes of law school, the professor addresses his neophytes with this combined warning and promise: "You come in here with a head full of mush, and when you finish—if you succeed—you will leave thinking like a lawyer."

To paraphrase: You open this book with a head full of false assumptions, but when you close it—if you have paid attention—you will think like an information genius and be able to find out just what you need to know.

1

The New Key
to Success

Why is being well informed important?

If you're like most businesspersons, you probably know your own industry inside and out. But it's less likely that you feel quite as well versed in the use and management of business information. And that is unfortunate, since in the 1990s and beyond it will be the companies that know how to use information that will emerge as winners.

What is "information consciousness," why is it so important, and how do you get it? First let's go over a few definitions. For our purposes, information is "meaningful data." Meaningful data is made up of numbers, statistics, scientific findings, new product sales trends, or any facts or series of facts that tells you something you didn't already know and adds to your understanding of whatever you are interested in finding out about. Pure data, on the other hand, is simply a number of facts without a significant relationship to any other data, e.g., Coca Cola's sales were $4 billion in 1990. But if you had that sales data plotted against other soft drink sales for 1990, then you'd have information. And while data leads to information, information leads to knowledge. And knowledge is the inexhaustible resource of the 1990s.

Why is information so vital in today's business environment? There are at least five interrelated phenomena driving its importance:

1. The ever–increasing speed with which business is conducted.
2. The need to monitor and follow competitors.
3. Changing demographics.
4. The globalization of business.
5. The increasing complexity of life.

Let's look at each of these factors separately.

The Pace of Business

It's obvious to any manager or executive that the pace of conducting business has in the last ten years or so accelerated from fast to faster to blazing. Personal-computer (PC) networks, fax machines, electronic mail, overnight delivery services, and other technological and social developments have made the speed of the business world increase at an incredible pace. Consider how slow it seems if a computer makes you wait a whole *five seconds* before completing a task. Or if your fax machine is out and you have to wait until *tomorrow* to receive a vital piece of correspondence. Clearly, we have "adjusted" ourselves and our ways to that of the silicon chip, and our expectations of how quickly we should have access to important information have been similarly affected. With companies exchanging critical data literally within seconds of its creation, firms that are unable to keep up will quickly be at an extreme disadvantage.

Monitoring the Competition

Related to understanding the pace of business is the increasing need to monitor competitive developments and competitors themselves. As the pace of business quickens, product release times shorten, research and development becomes more critical, and the need to monitor competitive conditions becomes more urgent. Case in point: In the early to mid 1980s, Xerox Corporation's famous copier business was getting brutally thrashed by the Japanese, who were able to introduce quality machines at much lower prices. Xerox, watching its main business rapidly becoming history, counterattacked and set up a competitor-monitoring system, studying in detail its competitors' manufacturing and distribution costs, staffing requirements, and other operational details. As a result, Xerox went back to the drawing board, redesigned its copier and operations, and today has regained much of that lost market share.

Monitoring competitive conditions and competitor activities has become so important, in fact, that today many Fortune 500 firms employ specific staff dedicated to that function. The Society of Competitive Intelligence Professionals' membership has grown from under 100 to over 1,600 in just over five years.

Changing Demographics

It's no secret that the country's population is getting older. The baby-boom generation has already entered its middle years and, beginning in the year 2000, will create a huge increase in the number of older Americans. Other significant demographic and social changes are occurring simultaneously: a new "echo" baby boom begun by women in their late twenties and early thirties, adult children living at home with their parents, and an increasing number of alternative households differing from the traditional two parents with children.

All of these shifts, of course, mean that the population will have changing behaviors, attitudes, and buying habits. Magazines like *American Demographics* make their living by tracking these changes and reporting on their significance to businesses and other groups who need to understand how the population of this country is changing. Businesses must keep up and understand these changes in order to succeed. And, of course, the way to keep up is by getting access to good information.

The Global Market

Not only must today's businesses be able to monitor competitive conditions and do so at an ever-accelerating pace, but they must also do so on a global basis. Of all the major changes in the way business traditionally has been conducted, the new global business environment is probably the most significant and critical.

While there have always been international business dealings and corporate conglomerates making deals, today's global business environment is different. Doris Walsh is publisher of *W-2 Publications* (Ithaca, New York), which publishes a newsletter that analyzes marketing strategies for Europe. She says that today all businesses should and must see their market as borderless. Conducting business on a global basis is a "new frame of mind."

What has brought about this new borderless way of conducting business? A number of major events and factors are responsible, some social, some technological, and some political.

First, there's the enormous impact of the communication technologies described above—faxes, PC networks, etc.—all of which have made it as simple and speedy to transfer data and information between countries as between offices. Accompanying this has been the overall "shrinking" of the world, as faster transportation and the power of the global media have brought everyone "closer."

No less significant is Europe's emergence, beginning in 1992, as one "single market" of 320 million consumers. This new unified market is the result of years of planning by the European Community member countries to eliminate regulatory, political, and other barriers that would impede trade between borders. This enormous effort has, in fact, created a single unified market that has become the object of intense attention and scrutiny of businesses around the world. Recent political movements in Eastern Europe toward a market economy have further spurred interest in international business. And on the other side of the globe, the emergence of the economies of the Pacific Rim countries (Japan, Korea, Thailand, etc.) has stimulated efforts and marketing in those nations by the United States' and other countries' businesses.

There has also been a strong effort mounted by the United States Federal Government to encourage American firms to sell overseas. For example, the United States Department of Commerce has established an Export Promotion Service to aid companies that want to market and advertise their products or services in other countries.

Now you might be tempted to say: "Okay, so the business world is global, but why does *my* business have to look overseas? I'm happy as a clam right here in the good old USA!"

But the rules of the game have changed. A global marketplace means that there is a new level of competition, and a whole new playing field with new rules. For example, Bausch & Lomb has seen its firm increase its revenues from markets outside the United States from 25 percent of total sales in 1984 to 37 percent in 1989. Diane Harris, vice president of Bausch & Lomb, in a recent talk warned businesses that "because a global competitor will have cost benefits of scale, technology access and multi-market hedging of risk, a company that cannot succeed globally is doomed to suffer in its home market as well, and perhaps not even to survive." Bausch & Lomb, in fact, created an entirely new International Division to pursue cross-marketing of products. Key staffers in the new division were empowered to enter into joint ventures, conclude licensing agreements, and cultivate acquisitions on their own initiative. More decision-making authority was granted to frontline managers working abroad.

Many businesses in other countries are, indeed, quickly taking advantage of this global marketplace. Japanese firms, in particular, are making very strong efforts. Harris said, "The Japanese know far more about what America's market needs are than vice versa . . . we need to know our competitors on a far deeper and more insightful level than we ever have before, because they know us as we have never been known before."

But just because you need to think and act globally doesn't necessarily mean that you're going to have an easy time of it. Marketing overseas is still a tricky operation, and requires a great deal of planning, foresight, and knowledge. To evaluate a specific country's potential, you need to find out about demand, competition, demographics, culture, and economic and legal barriers and regulations. And the commodity that's needed to pull all this off is *information*—a lot of information.

To successfully market and compete overseas, you need to know how to be able to obtain country profiles, foreign newspapers, overseas market research reports, government trade statistics, and data on legal barriers like price controls and profit repatriation. All of this data is *easily* available—if you have the information consciousness necessary to realize that you need the information and to know where you can find it.

The Increasing Complexity of Life

Today the world is more complex and, as a result, today's businessperson needs to be well-versed in a wide range of subjects. These subjects could run the gamut from the hazards of indoor air pollution to buying fax machines to knowing the laws on sexual harassment. You may find yourself needing to quickly become informed on a topic about which you have absolutely no prior knowledge. That's not a problem if you're an information-conscious executive and know where to quickly find the answers.

In summary, when considering the accelerating pace of business, competitive monitoring, and a global business environment, it's clear that we now operate in an "information economy." Alvin Toffler, in his book *Power Shift*, states that today knowledge *is* business, and that what is going to "count most" is knowledge about knowledge. And that's what this book is all about.

2
Never Assume Anything

If information consists of related facts, news, statistics, impressions, and so forth—pieces of intelligence that singly or jointly increase your awareness and build toward knowledge—then what is an assumption? It is a conclusion based upon none of those things. It is a guess, pure and simple—sometimes luckily true, but most often false. While in some cases it may be based on a knowledgeable intuition or a subtle understanding, most of the time it is based on nothing at all.

A book publisher we know decided awhile back to publish an anthology of in-depth articles concerning a profession with which he was very familiar. He reckoned that he needed only 30 meaningful pieces to make a fine book. Since there were probably 150 such articles published in any given year, it would, he assumed, be simple to acquire them, winnow the best, and write for permission to reprint. At a high monthly fee he retained a clipping service to find them. Three months and several hundred dollars later, he was dismayed to find nothing. He had made the *assumption* that such articles existed, because he thought that they should. Had he gone to a firm specializing in finding information, he would have learned this in ten minutes at a small fraction of the cost (more about this later).

But to have done the latter, it would have been necessary to sidestep his ego and ask a question rather than assume a fact.

People may choose to make assumptions for a variety of ill-founded reasons. Sometimes people make an assumption because they think they *should* know something. Another reason people may make an assumption is that they believe that they are the only one who has ever had this problem (or question), so they have no choice but to make an assumption. But in reality, it's more than likely that many others have had the same problem, and probably have even come up with the answers! Another reason people make assumptions is simply that they just don't know about the plethora of information resources that are available for the asking, and they feel that there's no choice but to rely on guesswork. Again, a bad methodology for coming up with a conclusion.

Don't feel too bad if you have made assumptions in your life. As any librarian or information specialist can tell you, most people are constantly making incorrect assumptions about the types and amounts of information available on a particular subject. One person may expect to find, say, statistics on a small town's soft-drink buying habits, but is then surprised to find out just how difficult such data can be to obtain; conversely, someone else may wonder how there could be anything "out there" on Japanese imports of compact disk players—and that data would be easy to find!

In order to make a good decision, that decision must be based on solid and reliable information. As the saying goes, you've got to do your homework! The alternative—decisions based on no information or on faulty assumptions—can lead to disaster.

To use an example from personal life, how many times have friends of yours complained that they went off on vacation only to be faced with transportation problems, overbooked hotels, wasted time, bad weather, or poor food and service? This type of thing rarely happens to people who are information conscious. When they decide to go somewhere, they do their homework. They have maps, they know weather statistics, they are armed with hotel and restaurant ratings, they've studied articles on the resort. They enjoy their vacation.

Why Do We Assume?

Why do many business executives make assumptions without finding and using information? There are a few main reasons.

First of all, there is no specific and solid education offered on the subject of information. For some reason, most business schools, while offering traditional courses on marketing and market research, haven't really kept up with the changing role of information and its uses outside of the traditional market research function. About the only type of professional that really gets a grounding in the information age and in strategic information-gathering is someone getting his or her masters in library science. The problem with most library science courses, however, is that they are usually narrowly structured to match the traditional library needs. But the business world has changed—and is changing—so quickly that a business's information needs are much more complex and strategic than what the traditional library school program provides.

Another reason why most executives are poor information finders is that most have had little actual hands-on experience in finding information. Most of us have some fuzzy memories of a grammar school introduction to the library: we were told how to use the card catalog, where to find the encyclopedias, and why we should keep our voices down. A fine introduction to the information age! And, unfortunately, that's about as far as most of us ever got; in fact, many a self-assured and successful businessperson is reduced to near helplessness when back in a library trying to find a piece of information. Often, after halfheartedly browsing through the card catalog and aimlessly wandering around the bookshelves, the businessperson "assumes" that there's no information on the subject, and walks out of the library disappointed.

Don't assume.

Ask Questions

What then is the key to getting information? Information is obtained by asking questions. *Lots* of questions. You start off with a "problem" of some kind, which could be anything: you could be the head of a company seeking to select a new plant site, a marketing executive looking for international sales opportunities, a health food store owner opening a new branch, or a consultant seeking new clients. All problems are different, but the process for uncovering information is the same:

- State the problem.
- Define what information you need.
- Determine why you need it.
- Decide what you will do with it.

One of the secrets to the proper understanding of information is the realization that the information you seek is almost certainly available. Not always, by any means. But the vast majority of the time, some information is indeed "out there" on the topic. The reason for this is fairly simple. You may think that your problem is unique, but it's actually much more likely that others have had the same questions and have done some leg work to dig up answers. The hard part of collecting and analyzing the data is likely already done—now all you have to do is find it!

Herein lies the most fundamental concept in information consciousness. At the risk of boring you, we'll repeat it: rather than making any assumptions that might lead to failure, make the assumption that the information needed for success is out there somewhere and available at a reasonable price. Then go look for it.

A few words of caution: Although it is very likely that the information you seek is already out there, there will be certain cases when it won't be. This is most likely to happen if your question is extremely narrow and specialized. So, for example, if you need to find out how many children under the age of eighteen live in Dallas, you are more likely to find that data than if you wanted to also know how many of those children prefer sugar to cake ice cream cones. The former is data that is collected by the government for statistical purposes; the latter is information you'd likely have to go out and collect yourself by creating a survey or hiring someone to do a survey for you.

Primary Versus Secondary Information

There is a very important distinction between primary and secondary information. Technically speaking, all information can be categorized as either primary or secondary. Primary information is derived directly from the original source providing the data. For example, a "focus group" interview, answers to a political survey, and observations from someone examining traffic patterns are all types of primary research. This is loosely equivalent to what you might call "firsthand" information. A secondary information source is one that takes that primary research and compiles it—often along with other information—in another source, often editing or recombining it with other data. So, for example, a textbook describing political surveys would be a secondary source. Books and magazine articles are also secondary sources.

There are other key distinctions between the two types of information. Secondary information is generally easy to find and is relatively inexpensive. Usually, it's just a matter of finding the right book, magazine article, government report, or published market study. However, if you find that there is no secondary information available, you may have to conduct your own primary research, which can be very expensive.

For example, say you were trying to get a feel for the market for laser printers. You would probably find a lot of secondary information on that topic, such as magazine articles, government statistical reports, and even "off-the-shelf" market research reports. These published reports are typically extensive studies of a defined market, providing key analysis and statistics on items like overall sales, leading companies, foreign competition, import/export figures, trends, technological impact, forecasts, and more. While these studies are not exactly cheap (ranging in cost from about $150 to over $3,000), they are a bargain compared to what you'd have to pay to get an equivalent custom primary study done to meet your needs. Primary research studies can cost anywhere from $10,000 to $50,000 or more. Note that although secondary market studies are normally more than adequate, there are cases when your data requirements are so very specialized or unique in some way that you would want to spring for a primary study.

Internal Versus External Information

Another key distinction between types of information is the difference between internal and external information. In a business context, internal information involves facts about your own company—your sales figures, the number of clients you have, where your products are shipped, etc. Internal information is used mostly—though not exclusively—for the purpose of measuring performance. External information, on the other hand, is information about the world outside your company. It involves facts about competitors, markets, demographics, environment, etc. External information is used mostly for planning and decision-making, although it is obvious that an effective decision to move into a new market, for example, should be based on a careful assessment of internal information (what markets we are in now) and external information (where are the opportunities). This sounds obvious, but apparently is not obvious to the vast majority of executives who make key decisions every day either without much external information at all, or without bothering to combine external information with internal.

Internal information is usually readily available to most of us, because its collection is vital and necessary for a business to operate. When Xerox and IBM talk about information, they are usually actually referring to internal information, because that's the kind of information their equipment is most useful in managing. It's also the kind of information most businesses *must* have.

External information is not usually perceived as being as important. It is more difficult to obtain, and is often neglected—with occasionally disastrous consequences.

The business press is replete with stories of companies and products that failed because changes in the marketplace or demographics—external information—were ignored or never perceived.

Those who inaccurately assume that their assumptions are correct may accurately assume that they, too, will fall by the wayside.

3

Translating Your Problems Into Questions

When the great Gertrude Stein was on her deathbed, a friend came to visit and found Ms. Stein in her final throes. Somewhat delirious, Ms. Stein kept repeating, "What is the answer? What is the answer?" Hoping to hear a final philosophic pronunciamento, her friend leaned forward expectantly. Gertrude Stein's final words were, "But then—what is the question?" Probably just a story, but it attests to the heightened information consciousness of that wonderful lady of letters.

What is your question? Oftentimes the question you ask is either obtuse or not the question you really mean to ask. And it's too often the case that you don't ask a question at all. But asking good questions is the key to getting the information you need.

Think about it. When you want a date, you need to ask if he or she is willing. If you feel you deserve a raise, you have to ask for it. And it's no less true that to get answers to your business problems, you have to ask. You *have* to ask questions. Contrary to what some may assume, answers don't magically appear out of the blue. Answers are the result of questions. And good answers are the result of asking good questions. Questions are keys, keys that unlock information vaults filled with answers.

But while it sounds simple, asking questions is not always easy. In fact, many of us have unfortunately been trained to avoid asking questions out of the fear that we will sound "stupid" or ask a "dumb question." In school, it seemed like the "nerd" was the one who always had his or her hand up asking all those annoying questions. Well, how much would you like to wager that today most of those nerds have carved out prominent and successful positions in their fields?

Even as adults, many of us shy away from asking questions. Some people will drive around, lost for hours, determined to "find it" themselves, instead of taking thirty seconds to ask a question and get on to the destination.

But it's the person who isn't afraid of asking a question, isn't afraid of how the question sounds, and isn't afraid of the tiny risk in requesting an answer who comes out on top. The old cliché that "there is no such thing as a stupid question" is very true: asking a question—any question—is simply a method or technique to get what you need. In this case, what you need is information, and you get information by asking questions. It's the key to improving your information consciousness.

If you don't have questions about your profession or your business or the ways in which you are conducting them, you should question that! It means you have a very low level of information consciousness. And you are not alone. When asked what is the single biggest sales resistance they encounter, the salespeople of a leading information and research service firm reported very simply that business executives say they have no questions!

Once you've convinced yourself that asking questions—lots of questions—is not only acceptable, but absolutely vital for getting what you want, you then need to know a little bit about the art of asking a "good" question. This doesn't mean that asking a "bad" question is stupid. It just means that some types of questions are going to be more fruitful in eliciting the most useful types of responses. But any question—no matter how "bad"—is better than not asking any question at all.

How do you go about coming up with good questions that will yield the answers you seek? The key is to know the procedures to follow. It's a thinking process and, like most techniques, there is a bit of an art to it.

Business Problems Are Information Problems

Interestingly, most executives will readily admit that they have plenty of problems. So the first step is to think of problems (and opportunities) as information needs, as series of questions that need to be answered. *Every problem that relates to a business or profession ultimately boils down to an information problem.* We think we have *decision* problems. But if we had a sufficient amount of information, all correct decisions would be indicated in that information. That's why it's so important, when thinking about problems, to think information. That's information consciousness.

All businesses have problems of one sort or another, even if they are not urgent ones. For example, here are some typical problems a business marketing a new baby food might have:

- Determining what type of customer to target.
- Deciding whether to sell the product overseas.
- Figuring out how to sell to customers in another country.
- Choosing between competing computer-system networks.
- Selecting a new product or service to introduce.
- Deciding how to price the product.

Now, if you say that you just don't *have* any problems, something isn't right! It means that you do not see any opportunities, areas for growth, or new horizons. And if that's the case, you really do have a problem—a big one—since it means you aren't moving forward. As Woody Allen told Diane Keaton in *Annie Hall*, "A relationship is like a shark—if it doesn't keep moving forward, it dies." The same is true for a business. Don't end up a dead shark.

Another reason for a low level of information consciousness is the lack of discipline in a logical progression of thought. Let's assume that you want to eat at a very fine French restaurant next Saturday evening. Lack of this discipline of logic would find you downtown that evening without a reservation, poking your head into a number of restaurants, checking prices and menus, being turned away by some, etc. In short, it would be a hassle.

The information-conscious reaction to this problem would be: My problem is to find a good French restaurant. So I need information about restaurants. Someone has probably had the same problem before. There is probably a guidebook on restaurants in this area. It may indicate which are French, plus facts on quality, prices, hours, atmosphere, and so forth. So if I find the guidebook, I solve my problem. Obviously, this is a simplified example. But the principle can be applied universally.

A young lady we know had a very typical problem. She needed to find a job. She had spent three years in a liberal arts college, then spent ten years in Italy married to an actor. While in Italy she became fluent in Italian and did some odd jobs translating, dubbing films, and so on. She later got divorced and returned to New York, desperately needing a job. She had no college degree, no office skills, and no real full-time job experience. For days she floundered around, visiting friends of friends who supposedly would help her and contacting employment agency after agency where all she was asked was how many words per minute she could type. Finally, she consulted our information-gathering firm. We applied some information discipline to the problem. The lady's assets included intelligence, language, affinity for the film business and other creative arts, and knowledge of Italy. The information steps required were:

- Get a list of all Italian companies with offices in New York. Contact them, giving priority to those involved in the arts.
- Visit the commercial attaché of the Italian consulate to find out what companies might be expanding or opening offices in New York.

- Find out which employment agencies specialize in bilingual jobs and which specialize in the music and film industry. Contact them.
- Get a list of companies in New York in the film, recording, artistic management, music, and television industries. Contact them.
- Get a list of all leading translation firms. Contact them.

The young lady found an excellent position.

In a business setting, the first step in following the discipline of logical progression of thought is to come up with a list of all your business "problems." The next step is to translate those problems into questions. This isn't really a very difficult task, and just requires you to "see" your problems in a different light and rephrase them.

So, for example, say that you were considering exporting a new type of baby food. Your business problems might be these:

- You need to know what type of persons would most want to buy your product.
- You need to know what regions of the world would be most receptive.
- You need to know why people in those regions would want to buy your product.
- You need to know what kind of computer system to get to organize your operations.
- You need to know why those buyers would choose your baby food over competitors' products.
- You need to know how much to charge for your product.

We could then translate these problems into preliminary questions:

- What are the demographics and purchasing habits of people who buy baby food?

- What countries have a need and a demand for this type of baby food?
- What are the demographics and cultural considerations of persons in those countries?
- What are my needs in a computer network? What do I want to be able to achieve?
- What do buyers of baby foods want that they currently aren't getting?
- What do competitors charge for a similar product? What will most people pay?

Here's another example. Say your problem was whether or not to sell frozen bagels in Europe. You could break this larger problem down into smaller, more answerable questions, and then subdivide those questions where possible. Here is a very simplified illustration.

Problem: *Should we sell frozen bagels in Europe?*

Now break this problem down into smaller questions.

Which countries are most likely to buy frozen bagels?

a. What are the demographics of people who buy this product?
b. Where can I find an analysis of demographics of various European countries?
c. Which countries' populations match up with those characteristics?

Say you've chosen France as a potential market.

What are the legal and regulatory requirements for importing food products in France?

a. Which United States government offices provide data and advice on selling overseas?
b. Which offices in France can tell me of their governmental requirements?

What is the competition like for frozen bagels in France?

a. What are the names of companies already selling this product?
b. Where can I find a market study analyzing sales and market shares for frozen bagels in France?

Breaking Problems Down

As you can see, the art of creating good questions means going through the process of breaking up a large, seemingly unmanageable problem into smaller pieces. Here are some other tips to help you ask for information in a way that will produce the best results.

❑ DETERMINE WHY YOU NEED THE INFORMATION

The reason behind any request is usually obvious. Yet a very clear and precise understanding of why information is needed is often lacking. For example, if you need a specific fact—like the 1988 sales of Perrier—to toss into a speech, you should ask for exactly that. Asking for a "run-down" on Perrier will increase the cost of the research, and may not even yield the sales figure you need. On the other hand, if you need background information to assess the market potential for a new kind of bottled water, then asking for a profile of the bottled water industry may be an excellent broad question. In any case, tell whoever is going to look for the answer why you need it. An understanding of the reason is vital to a successful search.

❑ TRANSLATE YOUR INFORMATION NEED INTO A QUESTION

Even when you've clearly established why you need information, formulating a good question can be a challenge. For example, say your company's sales compensation plan needs revamping. You want information to help you do it. You could ask for any available data on sales compensation plans. But such a request may produce huge masses of mostly useless information. Try asking instead, "Are there comparative studies of sales compensation plans that will tell me the norms for my industry?" This type of precise question could produce an equally precise answer.

❏ MAKE YOUR QUESTION SPECIFIC

Your real question could be a general one: "Will a branch office I am contemplating in Des Moines succeed?" Unfortunately, no one can answer this question as stated. But consider asking specific questions like: "What is the population of Des Moines?" "What is the political climate in that city?" "Who are my competitors there?" Combined answers to these questions, properly interpreted, will help you make an intelligent and successful decision.

❏ ASSESS THE VALUE OF YOUR QUESTION

Having a sense of the value of the information you need can help you phrase your question. Do you need the information for a low-priority idea you're working on? Did the boss ask for it? Is it related to a new $10 million product development plan? If you have some idea of the value of the information, you'll be better able to phrase your question and give critical guidance to a researcher. (You wouldn't want your secretary to spend a full day trying to find a hotel room in New York if there's only a 10 percent chance you'll go there.) More on the value of information in Chapter 4.

❏ DESCRIBE WHAT YOU ALREADY KNOW ABOUT THE ANSWER

You may already have part of your answer. For example, you want to know total United States distilled spirits sales in dollars, but you already have the figure in units. Or maybe there are some sources you've checked before without success. By all means, let your researcher know about the background information you have and where you've already looked. Much time is lost when people neglect to do this.

❑ DETERMINE THE AVAILABILITY OF THE INFORMATION YOU NEED

If you're not a researcher, you won't know what data is available and what is not. But a little careful thought on your part can tell you how likely it is that an answer will be found. For example, common sense should suggest that finding an already published marketshare breakdown of baby carriage sales for three counties in Idaho would be virtually impossible. Asking for a list of all the major department and discount stores in the top cities in Idaho is a question that probably can be answered, but common sense should suggest that it can't be answered in ten minutes.

❑ DO THE ASKING YOURSELF

Remember the telephone game? Ten people line up, and the first says a brief sentence to the second, who repeats it to the third, and so on. By the time the tenth person has heard the sentence, it has completely changed from what the first person said. If you have a question and want to get an answer, don't relay your request through a third party, like your secretary. Telling someone else to ask a question for you will almost insure that the answer you get will not be the one you needed. Always ask your own questions.

❑ DO YOU NEED AN ANSWER OR JUST A SOURCE?

This is an important distinction many people fail to make, especially when they are using someone else to perform their research. Generally, the more specific your question, the more you need an actual answer. If your question is very broad, you may wish to browse through the source yourself. In the example cited above, you might well need the answer to a specific question on population in Des Moines. But if a good fact book existed on the Des Moines area, you would want to examine that as well.

Typical Business Questions

Many people in business have told us that even when they are in a frame of mind to ask questions, they're not exactly sure what to ask questions about. They often feel that their particular problem or question doesn't relate to any information that may be available.

While we can't tell you what your own questions should be, we can dispel once and for all the notion that information may not be available. *You can and should ask questions about anything.* In most cases, information *is* available.

To suggest the endless possibilities, here's a sampling of how executives in various functions are getting results through asking questions:

- When the president of a major pharmaceutical company felt that he might have to justify his research-and-development expenditures at the next stockholder meeting, he asked for and got data on the research-and-development expenditures of ten similar firms.
- When back-up data was needed for the development of an electronics company's five-year plan, the planning director obtained information on typical industry financial ratios, articles on current management practices in the electronics business, data on exports, and a study of the industry's future in Europe.
- When the chairman of a major chemical company decided to look into potential acquisitions in the solar energy field, he

began by obtaining an overview report on the industry that identified three potential targets, two of which were later researched in depth.

- The marketing director of a company with a new bottled water subsidiary wanted to expand to Florida. He asked for a list of competitors in that state and then commissioned an in-depth study of the industry in Florida, including interviews with companies in the field.

- A sales manager scheduled an important meeting with a key prospect. Doing his "homework" beforehand, he dug for and unearthed vital facts on the prospective client, biographical details on the principals involved, and several published articles on the company and its industry.

- A disposable diaper firm became concerned about long-range sales forecasts. It collected birth-rate projection statistics through the year 2010 and used them to develop year-by-year data on the size of its potential market.

- A printing products manufacturer wanted to introduce a new line. He obtained an overview of the market, had an outside company research the alternative methods of distribution to end-users, and commissioned a survey of distributors. He was then able to competently determine his product introduction strategy.

- A public relations manager who needed to develop a campaign concerning diabetes figured that celebrities could help. He asked for and got a list of famous people who have the disease.

- A company president's son was seriously ill with a form of colitis. Instead of merely consulting the leading local specialist, the president first obtained a list of virtually every article published on the disease in medical journals over the past ten years. He then obtained copies of the articles, read them, and through them identified the four or five leading specialists on the disease in the world. He also obtained a background on the major drugs used to treat the disease. Then he took his son to the best doctors, armed with sufficient knowledge to discuss the case intelligently.

And here is just a brief sampling of requests recently handled for business executives by a qualified information-gathering firm, along with the reason behind each request:

- What was last year's consumption of imported beer in the United States? How much was imported from each country? (To establish a company's import guidelines.)
- What is the profitability of the health club business? (For an executive considering purchasing a franchise.)
- Are there any businesses with United States offices that specialize in the rental of ski chalets and apartments in Europe? (To find a way to plan a three-week stay at a ski resort in Switzerland.)
- What is the cat population of the United States? How many live in metropolitan areas? (To help plan distribution for a pet supply firm.)
- What were the top two songs of 1952? (For planning an anniversary celebration.)
- Please provide all demographic information on chain saw users—who uses them, where, and how often? (For a firm that produces a safety accessory.)
- The Indonesian government has new export regulations. What are they? (To help in the negotiation of an importing contract.)
- How do you spell the actual sound an owl makes? (For copywriting an advertisement.)
- Please obtain results of studies on the toxicity of benzoyl peroxide. (For assistance in complying with environmental regulations.)
- Please obtain a list of New York's richest men. (We thought this might have been for an ambitious single lady, but actually it was to help write a magazine article on expensive cars.)

- Who designed the L'eggs Panty Hose display rack? (For someone who needed a package design and liked this one.)
- Do food additives have any known adverse effects on child development? (For the public relations manager of a food additive company.)
- I need background on the industries and resources of one of the new republics that was formerly part of the Soviet Union. (For an executive who was scheduled to meet with the premier of the republic.)

Other questions that businesses frequently ask include:

- Where can I find demographic information on potential clients?
- How do my competitors distribute their product?
- Where can I find a suitable partner overseas for a joint venture?
- Is now a good time to get into this market?
- Are my customers satisfied with my product?
- What is the background of the new executive my competitor has appointed?
- What are the sales and revenues of the top companies in this industry?

Any questions?

4

The Price and Value of Information

What is information worth? How much should you be prepared to pay to get the facts you need? While most of us are conditioned to see the cost of something only in monetary terms, in the business and professional sphere it is necessary to equate cost with *value*. And the value of information is assessed by examining the time and money spent in acquiring it.

Time is precious. It is also finite. No matter how we try, we cannot increase it. No matter how much money we spend, we cannot gain more time.

Three factors must be considered when assessing the cost of information: time, money, and ultimate gain.

Information Is Never Free

Most of us think that public libraries and the information you find there are free. This is not really accurate. While it is true that the facts and data themselves may be "free" in that the resources are there for anyone to use, the gathering, collecting, and locating of information takes time; and time, as the saying goes, is money. Even for the most mundane tasks, there is a time cost in uncovering information. For example, if you need to fly to Seattle, and you or an aide spend two hours finding out all the flight and accommodation details, you will have used up valuable time; if instead you called a travel agency, the fee for that call would be the only cost factor involved.

It is incredible when you realize the number of important, high-salaried people involved daily in the drudgery of gathering information of one type or another. It's incredible because, first, the information has been gathered before and, second, it's available at a price. If you have raised your level of information consciousness sufficiently to be aware of these two things, then you are already halfway toward answering your question. Therefore, you have saved 45 percent of your time (money). This is true because, when there is an information problem, 90 percent of the work is in finding the sources, and 10 percent of the work is in using the source material to get the answer.

Here is another notion that blocks information consciousness. Many people believe that they must always do their own research to benefit from the information gained. This is normally *not* true, and can be very inefficient. Trying to find information on your own can be costly. In addition to the cost of your time, you must also add what is called the "opportunity cost." Let us assume that you hire someone whom you pay $20 an hour to do work for which you bill your clients $100 an hour. If that person does research for your own company's use, you would assume that this costs you $20 an hour. Right? Wrong! It costs you $120 an hour, because you are also losing the one hour of income that person would be producing. And it will probably take this person twice as long to get the information as it might take an information expert.

This is not to say that there is no point to performing some research on your own. In certain circumstances, for example when launching a new business or entering a new market, it is very important for the businessperson to do at least a little research in order to experience firsthand some intangibles, such as the "flavor" of the market being researched. This could be a matter of making just a half dozen phone calls to supplement the full research effort.

So information is *not* free, as there are various cost elements involved in locating and gathering it. But how much is the information actually worth? Ultimately, a piece of information's value depends on how much it aids you in making the best possible business decision. What's it worth to you to be able to make better decisions? You can't put an exact figure on it. But it's clear that better decision-making is what everything in business ultimately boils down to, and any resource that will improve decision-making is an extraordinarily precious one. Information is such a resource.

What's It Worth to You?

Things get tricky when we try to determine precisely how much a particular piece of information is worth, and to assign to it a specific dollar figure. Information's value is subjective. A piece of information may be worth exactly $1,000 to you, may be totally worthless to me, and may be worth $10,000 to the next person. Here are some illustrations of this point:

- The A.C. Nielsen Company does a continuous study that includes a measurement of the movement of different brands of corn flakes through supermarket outlets on a week-to-week and year-to-year comparative basis. This service sells for thousands of dollars per year. This study, needless to say, would be worthless to the owner of a "mom and pop" grocery store. It would be worth its price to a marketing consultant to the corn products industry. But it might be worth at least ten times its price to the Kellogg Company.

- The results of a survey done in October 1988 on the growth of the bottled water industry are available, let us say, for $100. The data is accurate and was compiled by a reputable firm. But there is a problem. The bottled water industry has been growing by leaps and bounds since 1988, and much has changed radically. If there has been no similar study since, your only alternative would be to conduct your own up-to-date survey at a cost of $20,000. What is the value of the $100 report? It would depend on (a) whether you have just a passing interest in bottled water, (b) whether you intend to open a million-dollar bottled water plant, or (c) whether you are an advertising agency on the verge of making your pitch to a potential account that bottles water. The $100 report is worthless to (a) because information must be acted upon to have value. It is also worthless to (b) because the information is too old to base a million-dollar expenditure on. It may have some value to (c) as background material to impress the prospective client.

- Let's border on the science-fictional and assume that it would cost $2 million to determine the number of bricks in all the buildings in Manhattan. Would anyone spend that kind of money for such seemingly worthless information? Yes—the used brick dealer who was just authoritatively informed by a seismologist that Manhattan will be totally destroyed by an earthquake within twelve months.

- Back to more mundane matters: The price of *The Guide to Restaurants* is $10. Would it pay to research the credentials of the author and the publisher? Not if you only intend to use it once for locating a restaurant. But yes it would, if you are a publisher contemplating issuing a competing book on that subject.

- It can cost $100,000 per year or more to set up, staff, and maintain an in-house library. Is it worth it? You can answer the question yourself now by simply asking this question: Worth it to whom?

So, like beauty, the value of information is in the "eye of the beholder." But assigning a particular value to information is even trickier when you consider that not only is information's value totally subjective, but it also depends, to a great extent, on the potential costs of *not* having that information. For example, not too long ago, a gentleman approached a research firm requesting patent search and engineering information on a new textile manufacturing process. As a result of the data, he was able to sell his product to Hanes Panty Hose for approximately $10 million. Without that information, as he later told the information service that uncovered the data, it would have been nearly impossible to have landed that contract. So, assuming that without the data he could not have made the deal, that information was worth $10 million! You need to try to figure out what the potential costs of not having the needed information could be. While in some cases it may not be much, in other cases you could easily be talking about thousands or millions of dollars.

Perhaps in part because the cost of information is difficult to define, the value of information is very subjective, and information itself is an intangible, many people confuse the value relationships involved. Either they believe they can get lots of information for a little money, or only a little information for a lot of money. They ask a question that they believe will cost little to answer, because the answer is of low value to them. Or they ask a question that they believe will cost a lot to answer, because the answer is of high value to them. In fact, as often as not, the low-value answer may cost a hundred times more than the high-value answer.

The Hard Costs of Information

How does the information-conscious person deal with this problem? First, you should never make a firm assumption about how much you *think* it will cost to obtain whatever information you seek. Second, always be prepared to accept that the information you want may not be available to you at a price you are able or willing to pay. Third—and most importantly—understand that virtually any question can be answered for $50, $500, $5,000, $50,000, or more. It all depends on how much time is spent looking, and on how much depth and detail is required. This is one of the most important concepts in the information field, because it can help you scale the level and cost of the research to the value of the answer to you.

Let's apply this concept to a specific problem and see what levels of information can be obtained, and for what situation each level is most appropriate.

Assume you are interested in a particular industry or market. It doesn't matter whether it's licorice, light bulbs, or lipstick. Here's a rough idea of the information you might get at the various cost levels:

- *"Free" (a call to the library).* Not truly free—your taxes have paid for the library, and you must use your time to place a call or make a visit. The librarian might be able to look up a trade association's address and phone number for you, or read a statistic out of a popular handbook like the *United States Industrial Outlook.* This approach is obviously suitable only when you just need a readily available single fact, or if you are prepared to spend a lot of time in the library.

- *$50–$250.* For this amount of money, you could do your own online search or hire a research firm for an hour's work and obtain a few statistics on the market, find a few trade magazine articles, or get names of leading companies in the field. This approach is useful when you need quick general information or a brief consultation.

- *$500–$1,000.* In this cost range, you should be able to get a more comprehensive overview of the industry, based on a gathering of readily available secondary data. A reasonably comprehensive—but not exhaustive—search of published literature would be included. Major articles from trade journals, basic government statistics—essentially anything that has been collected and published. All of this could be useful for background information, speech making, report writing, and early stages of planning and problem solving.

- *$5,000–$10,000.* Based on the secondary information gathered above, plus more exhaustive searching and limited telephone contacts with trade sources, a 20- to 100-page profile of the industry could be prepared in this cost range. The profile would cover the size of the market, companies in the field, distribution patterns, regulations, etc., though not with the depth and detail of the next level up. It would also be useful for the initial stages of studying an opportunity, a new product, a new venture, or an acquisition.

- *$15,000 and up.* At this level, a full-scale industry and market study can be produced. It would include a fully exhaustive search of secondary data; extensive interviews with trade sources, manufacturers, retailers, and other industry components; careful study of market potential and other factors affecting the industry—all embodied in a report, with summary and analyses, that might run up to several hundred pages. In these higher price ranges, a customized survey of consumers (whether individuals or other businesses) would be included. This type of in-depth study is essential for all advanced stages of planning, product introductions, acquisitions, and so forth.

Types of Information-Providers

Another way to perceive the cost-value problem is to look at the broad categories under which information can be obtained from the vast array of publishers and information-gathering organizations. Although it may be difficult for you to determine exactly how much a particular piece of information is worth, those who sell information must indeed do just that and come up with a hard price. Different types of information-providers have created different methods for pricing their information services. The following types are listed in order of least to most costly.

❑ ONLINE DATABASE PROVIDERS

Producers of online databases charge an hourly rate, based on the amount of time the user spends electronically connected to their system. Rates vary quite a bit, but typically run about $60–$150 per hour of online search time, with an additional cost added for each item retrieved (this may range from 10¢ to $10 or more per item). But in this case, remember, it is your time that you are spending doing the search, and there is no human "expertise" being bought—just the ability to quickly access and search already collected data. For more details on locating information from online databases, see Chapter 7, which is devoted to this subject.

❏ PUBLISHED STUDIES

Sometimes information has already been gathered and put into printed form, with a set price established by the publisher. The publisher generally tries to establish a competitive price based on what others are charging for similar reports, and on what the market will bear. There is a wide price range for published market studies and reports. Typically they cost anywhere from $100 to $300 for the smaller ones and from the low to mid thousands for large and detailed studies.

❏ MULTICLIENT STUDIES

A special category of published reports is "multiclient studies and surveys," which are "sponsored" in advance, usually by a limited number of organizations. The sponsors can then request additional, highly specific questions they want answered as part of the study. This makes multiclient studies more useful to them than ordinary published studies. In the case of consumer surveys, multiclient studies are often referred to as "syndicated research."

❏ INDIVIDUALLY CONTRACTED STUDIES

These are ordered and paid for by a single entity, to whom the results belong exclusively. "Custom" studies and surveys of this kind may, of course, fall within a very broad price range, depending on the information needed, but typically are the most expensive type of information that can be obtained, as they often involve extensive primary research.

The special types of firms that carry out these contracted searches for information are called information-gathering services. Many of the smaller ones call themselves "information brokers"—independent firms that perform research for a fee. Reva Basch, president of the Association of Independent Information Professionals, explains that information brokers sell their expertise in knowing how to locate information, and not the end result. In fact, when you engage the services of such a firm, you do not know what the results will ultimately be. Occasionally, an information search may even turn up "nothing" at all. But the fact that there is nothing on a topic could be of great value in certain instances (e.g., an inventor who wants to find out if there are already any published references to his new product idea). So when you hire someone to locate information for you, you generally do not pay for the actual data uncovered, but for the time and expertise required to find it. Information-gathering firms and brokers typically charge an hourly rate ($50–over $150) plus any direct costs incurred.

The foregoing example should suggest points that cannot be repeated too often:

- Information that has already been published somewhere is much less expensive than information that must be gathered and developed on a customized basis.
- "Raw" information (a bunch of statistics from a book or copies of articles) is much less expensive to provide than any kind of written summary or report based on that information.
- In the case of large studies and surveys, it is always cheaper to purchase "off the shelf" than to contract for customized research.
- The more important the use to which the information will be put, the more exhaustive a research job should be done.

- Collecting secondary (published) information is much less costly than conducting primary original research.

Failure Costs

At this point you may say to yourself, "You've told me that information is not free, and you've told me something about its cost and value. But how do I know when it's really worth spending money for?"

The answer is that you may never know, because the true value of information is often measured only in relation to the cost of the failure that results from not having it.

We once knew two salespersons who worked for the same company. They sold the same line of products to the same types of customers in similar territories. They both had the same background and experience.

Yet John, the first salesperson, earned close to $80,000 a year, while Harry, the second, only managed to earn $40,000 a year. Harry was a good dresser, a smooth talker, and a hard worker who wined and dined his customers regularly. He was, in fact, a good salesperson. In an attempt to find out why John was twice as successful as Harry, the sales manager visited John at his home. There, in his basement office, was a veritable Library of Congress. There were complete files on each of John's customers. For each company, he kept records on its history, earnings, and plans. He had tear sheets of its advertisements and notes on its marketing practices. He had information on each of his customer's problems. There was even a complete rundown on the executives he contacted within those companies—their hobbies, family, club memberships, and the like. In short, John had a lot of information; Harry had very little. The information was worth $40,000 to John; the lack of it cost Harry at least $40,000.

A good way to measure the value of information comes from an older, but still valid and enlightening, article in the May 15, 1976, issue of *Boardroom Reports*, which makes a comparison of "failure costs." According to that study, the likelihood of the failure of a $100,000 project is one in three without research, so the failure cost is $33,000. With research, the risk of failure is one in five, for a failure cost of $20,000. The value of the research is then the difference between the two costs, or $13,000.

In summary, information is not free. It takes time and resources to gather it. The value of a piece of information depends on the circumstances, and on the potential costs of not having that information. There are different ways of obtaining information, and the cost of each level of information service varies. The key is to match your need with the appropriate level.

5

How to Judge the Quality of the Information You Get

Back in the early 1980s, if you picked up any of a handful of market research studies on the emerging home "videotext" industry, you would have read that the industry was poised to explode during the decade and experience tremendous growth. And, after reading such reports, you might have decided to enter that market, or invest in a company in that field. However, the only thing that home videotext experienced during the 1980s was a spectacular *lack* of growth. And any business that decided to enter that market based on those forecasts most likely ended up losing money.

So far this book has examined the importance of having information consciousness and of asking good questions. But another vital issue is determining information reliability and believability. Although we are, indeed, in an "information age," and surrounded by data and facts of all kinds, separating the good information from the bad is not necessarily an easy task.

You can see that this is true not only in the business world, but in day-to-day personal life as well; for example, in the new forms of "news" called infotainment and docudramas, it's nearly impossible to determine where the facts end and the fiction picks up. And it seems almost impossible to decide which of the latest scientific studies to believe. Does eating oat bran lower cholesterol? Is drinking two cups of coffee a day okay? Clearly, more information doesn't always mean clearer information, or ultimately make it easier to make decisions.

In today's business arena, scores of competing data sources are being created and churned out by a wide variety of firms. The developers of these information sources, like other vendors, make claims of having the best, most complete, or most useful "product." But completeness and quality vary between sources, and the well-known warning of *caveat emptor* applies to buyers of information, just as much as it does to buyers of other goods. Information has become another "commodity," and you, the customer, must be alert to its quality and reliability.

In addition to distinguishing good data from bad, today's smart information users need to have the ability to properly interpret and analyze data. Misreading what data is telling you can be just as dangerous as having no information at all. Just remember what happened to American car manufacturers in the early 1980s when they misjudged consumer demand for smaller and more fuel-efficient cars!

No Source Is Perfect

What are some of the most common quality and reliability problems in business information sources? You might be surprised to discover that even supposedly "unimpeachable" sources can contain errors, be misleading, or be misinterpreted. Take, for example, the "bible" for United States statistics, the *Statistical Abstract of the United States*. Some years ago the volume contained several critical number transpositions. And if you don't read the fine print on how to use the data—and honestly, how many of us really do?— it's very easy to misunderstand such vital things as units of measurement, years covered, and other key supporting data that you must understand in order to know what you're really reading!

So the first thing you should be aware of is that no source is perfect, and that you should never assume that the data you have obtained is necessarily correct. The simplest and best method for checking reliability is to consult a second or even a third source. Now, of course, if there are no other sources, you will have to rely on the particular source you are using—however, there are still other methods you can use to help ascertain the reliability of a unique source, as described at the very end of this chapter.

Although it is true that you should never assume any single source is perfect, it is also true that some types of sources are more likely to have reliability problems than others, and that some data quality issues are of highest importance. A description of some of these "high profile" information quality areas follows.

❏ COMPANY DIRECTORY DATA

One of the data sources most commonly used by businesses are company directories. Company directories list key facts on businesses, such as their address, total sales, names and titles of key officers, products and services produced, and so on. Some directories have even more information, such as market share, profit and loss statements, subsidiary linkages, and so on. These are vital research tools that are used regularly by almost all business researchers. Some of the most well-known directories include *Dun & Bradstreet Million Dollar Directory, Standard & Poor's Register of Corporations, Directors, and Executives,* and *Ward's Business Directory.* These can normally be found in print form, as well as online.

Unfortunately, while these are immensely valuable guides, they can be filled with inaccuracies. Typos, outdated information, and poor data collection methodologies all are causes of frequent errors.

There are a number of reasons why. One, according to sources within the industry, is that for a variety of motivations, ranging from tax purposes to establishing of credit, an owner of a business will sometimes overstate or understate sales figures. Unlike the Securities and Exchange Commission, a directory publisher has no legal recourse should a firm provide false data. Probably even a more common source of bad data is the directory publisher's failure to update old information. Smaller, private, and lesser-known firms receive less attention from directory providers, and there are likely fewer checks on data accuracy—though big mistakes can occur with larger firms, too. A while ago, we performed a computer search to locate presidents of major companies, and found that the computer database listed a secretary at Canon as the firm's president; and for Eastman Kodak the database listed one of the company's marketing directors as the president! The sad thing is that such incidents are not all that unusual.

❏ MARKET SIZE AND FORECAST REPORTS

Like company directories, market size and forecast reports are frequently used by business, but are also frequently wrong! These reports, which are issued by various well-known—and not so well-known—research firms, all purport to measure the size of a particular industry or product, and frequently forecast growth into the future as well. So, for example, such studies might tell you things like how many home healthcare diagnostic kits were sold last year, or the expected number of CD-ROMs to be sold through the year 2000, and so on.

However, measuring the market size of an industry or product is a tricky business—and forecasts are even trickier! Let's look at a study that attempts to measure the number of laser printers sold last year. The key question, of course, is where is the publisher going to find this information, and how is it going to make a count? There are a variety of methodologies that can be used, some more reliable than others. Most rely on a sample survey of some kind, and these may be conducted in a variety of ways. Some try to talk to buyers and measure placements by analyzing the demand side, but a more reliable method is to survey manufacturers and measure the supply side. There are other ways in which survey methodologies differ, e.g., whether the survey is conducted by mail or by phone, and whether the sample is truly representative of the population being measured. Other important issues relate to what type of person answers the survey, and whether that person truly has the knowledge and ability to provide accurate answers.

As uncertain as market size measurements are, forecasts are even more so. When it comes right down to it, you have to remember that a forecast is really nothing more than a guess. Now some guesses are going to be more educated than others, and some will be based on better information than others, but predicting the future is not exactly one of the hard sciences. Just ask any meteorologist!

The best forecasters have a track record in successfully measuring the specific items being studied and a complete understanding of the product, industry, or whatever else is being measured. A good forecaster tries, as much as possible, to take into account any upcoming technological, sociological, and demographic trends that could impact growth. And, importantly, a good forecast provides not just figures and tables, but lots of explanatory text that describes the underlying assumptions and methodologies, and shows the user how best to use the information presented.

❏ POLLS AND SURVEYS

Polls and surveys are notoriously unreliable. Conducting a proper poll or survey of people's opinions or habits is a true science that demands a high degree of knowledge about technical issues like random sampling error, non-sampling errors, non-response errors, and more. Some popular surveys, such as magazine reader surveys, are conducted in flagrant violation of these rules, and their results, consequently, can be virtually worthless as any true measurement of people's opinions or behaviors. Other polls may make some effort to avoid the most obvious accuracy problems, but still end up with such a large margin of error that relying on their results is, at best, extremely risky.

In addition to poor data collection and measurement methods, polls and surveys can suffer from a variety of other problems:

- Organizations with a specific agenda can word questions to elicit desired responses or interpret results in a manner to serve their aims.
- Placement of questions can impact respondents' answers.
- Choice of words and "loaded" phrases can influence respondents' answers.
- People often knowingly or unknowingly give wrong answers, due either to faulty memory or a reluctance to provide honest answers. People are particularly prone to providing incorrect answers to sensitive questions, or ones that they perceive as reflecting badly on them.

The best advice we can provide on using polls and surveys is to always confirm any results by checking other sources, and not to rely on them alone in making any major business decisions.

Other Information Quality Problems

The following are other factors that can trip up business information users.

❏ BIASED INFORMATION

When reading any report, study, or article, always find out who sponsored the report, why it was issued, and what the aims of that sponsoring organization are. Whose "ox will be gored" by the publication of such data?

❏ NEWSPAPERS

Daily newspapers operate under the heat of a deadline, and errors can and do occur. Newspapers have a tendency to "overinterpret," and of course occasionally to sensationalize findings of a single study or incident. For example, the recent Boston study that found that oat bran did not lower cholesterol was played up as the new definitive conclusion on the matter when, in fact, it was only one of a number of serious studies whose findings are still being debated.

The New York Times is considered an authoritative newspaper. But say, for example, that it publishes a figure for United States sales of soft drinks in an article about Coca-Cola. That figure may come to be taken as gospel and be reprinted in other publications, even though the reporter writing the article may have obtained the figure from the National Soft Drink Association, which may well have conducted a poor study. Many associations publish figures about the size of their industry, and these are sometimes the only figures available. Yet those figures often come from a poll of the association's members, which may have been conducted unscientifically, or may suffer from the fact that the respondents may not have the incentive to answer with complete candor.

❑ OUTDATED INFORMATION

Is the information provided by the source up-to-date? Is it first- or secondhand? How did this source actually come up with this information? These are all key issues that reflect on the reliability of the source. To take a very simple example, the recognized authoritative source for demographic information is the United States Bureau of the Census. The data is firsthand information, obtained through exhaustive survey procedures (complaints about certain undercounts notwithstanding). Yet, the last census prior to publication of this book was completed in 1990, so the data, while from an authoritative source, will be a few years old by mid-decade. Unfortunately, aside from periodic, limited updates and projections, there are no real alternatives.

❏ ONLINE INFORMATION

It might seem to some people that information found online via computers is more trustworthy than other information. This is nonsense. Data found via computer is at least as likely to contain errors as information found in print. For more information on computer databases, see Chapter 7.

❏ MASSAGED INFORMATION

Finally, the manner in which information is presented can significantly affect your use of it. Most information that has been assembled from statistics, data, facts, etc., has been "massaged" in some way before it gets to you. Massaging is the putting together of data in a manner that applies to a particular problem at hand. For example, let us assume that information concerning birth statistics in Indiana is required. Many different types of such statistics may be available from several different federal, state, and local agencies. Gathering all of these statistics together, it may become necessary to create charts or graphs (or both) to make the data intelligible. If ten people created charts from the same set of statistics, we would have ten different charts. This is because each person would "massage" the information in a different way. All the different charts may be correct, yet the way the information is presented will affect how the data is interpreted.

Say, for example, you wanted to know total dollar sales of widgets in the United States in 1989 and 1990. You might be shown a simple table like this:

1989	1990
$175,000,000	$182,000,000

Or, using the same data, you might be presented with a table like this:

(Millions of dollars)

1989	1990	% Increase
$175.0	$182.0	3.8%

The second table is not only easier to read, but it presents more information using the exact same data. Reading the first table, you might quickly grasp that widget sales were up by $7 million, but you might miss the fact that the increase was only 3.8 percent—*less* than the inflation rate for that year.

Proper and accurate interpretation also depends upon your own abilities of perception. Always bear your original question in mind and pay close attention to such things as scales and legends on graphs and charts.

To continue our example, assume you commission a study of the widget industry. The researcher you assign to the project returns with a graphic representation of the trend in widget sales at the National Widget Company. (See Figure 5.1.) Initially, you're not likely to pay too much attention to the scale on the graph. You'll look at it and see widget sales trending down slightly. A different researcher doing the same graph could use exactly the same data and present it on a graph with a different scale. (See Figure 5.2.) Now you take a quick look at the graph and exclaim, "Widget sales are crashing!" The difference in your perception is caused by the scale of the graph. Obviously, data can be manipulated to suit anybody's purpose.

Always use your intelligence and common sense. Assume you wanted information on the microprocessor industry. You can't afford to commission a study, so you ask if one has already been done and is available in published form. Say you find a study, and it's "only" one year old. But if you know anything about the industry, you'll know that in a year's time, the industry and products change drastically, and so the study would only be of limited value.

The main point to keep in mind is to always be skeptical when using information. Here is some basic advice to better

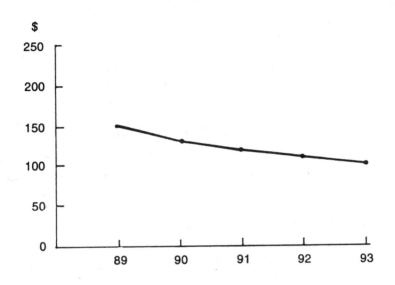

Figure 5.1 The National Widget Company's sale of widgets depicted on a graph using a scale of $0–$250 million.

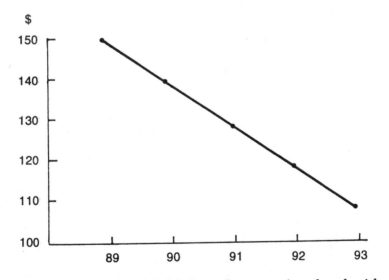

Figure 5.2 The National Widget Company's sale of widgets depicted on a graph using a scale of $100–$150 million.

insure that the information you use is accurate and trustworthy:

- Know your subject. The more you know about the topic you're researching, the less likely it is that you'll be misled by bad data.
- Talk to people. When you find pieces of data in print or online, treat them as leads, not as final answers. Run the data by some knowledgeable persons and get feedback.
- Use more than one source, if possible, to compare data.
- If you have questions about data, call the provider and ask him or her to identify the original source of the data. Ask about data collection techniques. Are you satisfied with the answers you got?
- Track down authors of articles and market studies, and interview them. You'll get clarifications and analyses not provided in the published piece, and will get your own questions answered.
- Don't pay too much attention to forecasts. Remember what they are—guesses!
- Always check footnotes, units of measurement, explanatory material, etc. Sometimes, the smaller the print, the more significant it is.
- When reading a study or analysis, find out the purpose of the publication or sponsoring organization. Is it purely to collect and publish data, or are there any political, ideological, or other agendas?
- If your goal is to insure as high a degree of accuracy as possible, use primary over secondary sources.
- Try, as much as possible, to obtain skills, knowledge, and training in the field you are researching.
- Cultivate the art of critical thinking. Don't accept what you read as gospel. Get confirming sources, ask questions, talk to experts, probe for motivations, and use your intuition—if something just doesn't sound right, check it out further.

Finally, remember that unused information is useless. An encyclopedia is worthless if never referred to—as is any dictionary. So many professionals and business people subscribe to much-needed trade literature and even commission studies and surveys without ever glancing at them! Then there are those who read the information, but never use it. To be of value, information must be acted upon. If it is ignored, it is valueless. Too busy? If your competitors find time to take advantage of the world of information, you will soon find yourself with nothing to be busy about.

6

Welcome to the Age of Information

Okay everybody, put down what you're doing! Look ahead, take note, stand up, pay attention! The "information age" has arrived! From this day forward, your lives will forever be changed!

Such is the sense of drama that usually accompanies a description of the new information environment. But what does that catchy "information age" phrase really mean? Few of us actually stop to think about what an information age is and what it means to live during such a time.

In general, it means that information has become the major force propelling society. It is the fuel that turns the wheels of modern business and modern living, and makes them "run." Let's look a little closer at how this all came about.

Information itself, of course, is hardly anything new. The storing and sharing of knowledge has been going on since before humans started writing on stone and papyrus. A giant leap forward occurred when the printing press was invented, as it allowed facts to be easily communicated to anyone at virtually any place. From that time, up until about the middle of this century, people found information either by going to a library or by purchasing encyclopedias and other reference

books. Later, they were able to utilize special information services, such as Dun & Bradstreet's credit reporting services,
which actually started before 1900.

The Computer

Then, in the middle of the twentieth century, a number of
developments occurred that helped create today's new information environment, or information "age."

The most significant of these developments was the inven-
tion of the computer. The computer brought tremendous advances: it massively increased the amount of information that
could be collected and stored; provided the power to combine,
edit, and synthesize collected data; and made it simple to
provide instantaneous transmittal of data to anyone anywhere
who had access to a computer terminal.

At the same time, society's need for information accelerated
rapidly. The world became more complex: disciplines grew
increasingly narrow and specialized; heavy industry gave way
to services and knowledge-based businesses; communications
and transportation advancements brought together people and
their ideas from around the world; and an international emphasis on technology spurred a faster race for scientific and technical data. Each of these phenomena fed off the other, creating
a spiraling demand for more information on more topics—to
be delivered much faster.

In response to this ever-growing demand for facts and data,
traditional book and magazine publishers geared up and began
producing more information, and in additional formats (e.g.,
microfilm, computer tape). At the same time, firms other than
traditional book and journal publishers entered the business of
producing information; many of these specialized in providing
data via computer tape, or remotely, "online."

The United States government, as it expanded its roles and
services during the 1950s, 1960s, and 1970s, became an enormous producer of all kinds of information, ranging from highly

technical and scientific reports and journals to consumer advisories to business development guides—and countless other documents. Companies and organizations set up in-house information services departments and computer networks in order to collect, manage, and disseminate all this external—as well as their own internal—information, so as to make better decisions.

The Information Industry

All of this information activity gave rise to a new "information industry," which is composed of a variety of subdisciplines and segments. To get an idea of the types of businesses that are an integral part of the information industry today, consider the following list, which names just some of the leading organizations in the field:

- *Association of Independent Information Professionals.* This is an organization of independent firms that sell information-finding services. These information-gathering firms are also known as "information brokers."
- *Association of Information Managers.* This association consists of information managers and executives in corporations and government dedicated to advancing the information management profession.
- *American Society for Information Science.* This is an organization composed of individuals interested in the science and theory of information technology and related topics such as storage and retrieval of data.
- *Information Industry Association.* Members of this organization include the very largest of the information companies, e.g., AT&T, Dun & Bradstreet, Knight Ridder, McGraw-Hill, etc., and are concerned with "macro" issues affecting their industry, such as governmental regulations, competition, new technology, and so forth.

- *Society of Competitive Intelligence Professionals.* Individuals who belong to this group perform "competitive intelligence" for their companies, and their duties include gathering data on competitive conditions, monitoring competitor activities, and so forth.
- *Special Libraries Association.* This organization is composed of librarians who do not work in a "traditional" library setting. Many corporate librarians and "information specialists" belong to this group.

The Information-Gathering Field

Who are the people that belong to these groups? What sorts of jobs are directly linked to the information industry? Since virtually everyone's job involves finding, managing, and disseminating information, it's no exaggeration to say that everyone is involved in some way in the information industry. But there are certain jobs that are directly and exclusively devoted to the information field.

Probably the most visible of these jobs is the librarian, or more specifically in business, the company or corporate librarian. Although company librarians have been around for a long time, because of the enormous changes in the use and management of business data, during the last ten years or so corporate librarians' jobs and duties have changed. In fact, many of them no longer even call themselves librarians, but instead prefer other titles like "information manager" or "information specialist." Such titles better reflect the varying and more sophisticated roles of today's corporate librarian, who almost always performs such tasks as computerized database searching and, in some organizations, strategic monitoring and collection of information on specified industries and companies, as well.

A number of individuals who have had traditional library education and experience have left their field and set up their own information brokerage (also called information-gathering) firms, through which they sell their expertise at finding information and searching online databases. Many businesses that do not have expertise in locating facts or performing searches hire information brokers to do the job for them.

While many of these information brokerage firms are small—sometimes consisting of a single individual—there are a few notably larger ones. Our firm, FIND/SVP of New York City, perhaps the largest and most well-known of these, has more than 11,000 users nationwide, revenues of nearly $20 million, and a staff of 175. We provide quick consulting and research by telephone, as well as a variety of other information-gathering and business intelligence services.

Many companies have created new staff positions just to take advantage of the new information environment. For example, most Fortune 500 firms today have employees whose duties relate specifically to finding information on competitors and competitive conditions. This new field has given itself the name "competitive intelligence" to describe its function. Typically, persons involved in this field perform strategic monitoring of key data sources such as online databases, government filings, Securities and Exchange Commission reports, and other sources of facts and insights on the competition. Depending on the particular "culture" of the firm, a competitive intelligence function could be located within the library, strategic planning, marketing, or market research departments.

Another recently created position is the CIO, or Chief Information Officer, who is the person in charge of a company's entire information resources. These resources usually include management information systems and electronic networks. In recent years this position has received a good deal of attention as an emerging new job in the information industry.

Other jobs directly involved with information are those held by market researchers. These people are typically responsible for a wide variety of data-gathering and analysis operations, including both quantitative and qualitative surveys.

Finally, there are the producers and resellers of all this sought-after information. These include traditional book and magazine publishers, organizations and institutions that gather and sell facts and information of special interest, database creators that put all that information into electronic searchable formats, and online "hosts" that resell and distribute the database producers' products. For more information on the online database industry, see Chapter 7.

A Sampling of Resources

The new information environment has emerged so quickly that few have learned how to use it. Yet it has changed the way sophisticated companies and executives do business. Here are a few examples of what this new information environment means to businesses:

- If you want to know about something, the fact that it can probably be found is not so farfetched when you realize that a summary of virtually every major article in the business press published in the past five years is stored on computer and readily retrievable in the space of a few minutes.
- If you sell to consumers, there is a wealth of consumer purchasing-power statistics readily available, including a myriad of breakdowns by zip code.
- Are you looking for new suppliers overseas or keeping tabs on competitive importers? There's a computerized service that keeps track of imports into the United States for various commodities by country and port of origin, port of arrival, and consignee!
- Want to pinpoint your marketing? Simply select the industry you market to, the size of the company that makes the best customer, the title of your typical buyer, and the zip codes where you'd like to sell. A printout of prospective customers' names can be on your desk within minutes.
- Need to find a manufacturer or retailer in a certain region of the country? Today the entire country's yellow pages can be

searched on a single computer CD-ROM disc. (See page 108 for a description of CD-ROMs.)

- Want key facts on a company you're researching? All public companies must file extensive financial reports with the Securities and Exchange Commission in Washington, DC. All of those statements and supporting documents can be accessed in seconds.

- Want to sell your product in other countries? The United States government has set up an entire department within the Department of Commerce devoted to providing free and cheap information to businesses that want to sell their products or services overseas.

- Looking for the right consumer? The Bureau of the Census sells a geographical mapping system called "TIGER" that can pinpoint by zip code the exact demographic characteristics of the neighborhoods you want to reach.

- Want to check out whether a patent has been filed on a new product? Patent and trademark searches can be done from the comfort of your computer terminal.

- If you need to track news developments around the world, you can choose from a handful of international news wires that are updated every fifteen minutes.

- Need to see how your investments are performing today? Financial markets and stocks can be tracked minute by minute in "real time."

- Worried about competitors in Europe or Japan? If you need to check facts on foreign competitors, full-blown statistical and analytical reports are ready for your review.

The above list doesn't even begin to scratch the surface of the types and amounts of information available today for the asking. In fact, for many people, all of these wonderful data resources have caused the "information overload" problem we briefly mentioned in the introduction of this book.

It is true that there is now such an enormous amount of facts, data, statistics, reports, and studies being produced and disseminated that businesses can easily feel overwhelmed and even paralyzed. For some, there's so much "out there" that the job of deciding which source to utilize becomes a confusing and overwhelming task. That's why it is so vital that businesses become information-conscious, learn about the information environment around them, and discover how to search for answers. Such knowledge, while not eliminating the possibility of having an "information anxiety" spell, will provide you with the confidence and skills you need to best understand and utilize information.

Future Resources

If we peer just a bit into the future, we can get a glimpse of some fascinating developments expected to occur in the information industry. For example:

- Instead of the slow, manual key-in process that many database producers use to convert "hard copy" data to online form, the increasing sophistication and reliability of scanners and bar code readers will speed the process and help further digitalize tons of data now in hard copy form. Everything from the White House budget to the papers in your file drawers are candidates for a quick conversion to digital format.

- As the business and information world becomes even more international, additional data from non-United States sources will become more available. This will expand the "information explosion" even further and will present increased opportunities for those who know how to selectively use this information.

- Automated language translation devices are another upcoming development. Sometime in the not-too-distant future you may, for example, be able to access a Japanese document directly online from Japan, and then have your computer instantly translate the report into English.

- New ways of manipulating and organizing information are being experimented with and evaluated. For example, "hypertext" software organizes and links different kinds of information together in a non-linear manner. Users of hypertext jump from topic to topic in an "associative" manner that supposedly is more akin to the way people think. Hypertext is expected to find a strong niche in emerging multimedia applications—software that can combine and manipulate text, graphics, video, animation, and audio in a single program.

- Another example of information manipulation is "custom publishing." In 1990, the publisher McGraw-Hill, in a joint venture with R.R. Donnelley printers and Eastman Kodak Company, developed a system that could produce "customized textbooks." Educators can select specific sections of a textbook based on their particular needs, and combine it with their notes and other items to create their own customized book. This electronic system can even repaginate and create a customized table of contents.

Data Privacy

Not everything on the information industry horizon is bright and rosy, however. One issue of growing sensitivity is "data privacy." Credit bureaus, marketing companies, and other firms that make their living by collecting and selling data about people are finding that the public is becoming increasingly disturbed by unwanted intrusions into their private matters. For example, after privacy objections were voiced, a major information-provider, Lotus Corporation, recalled a planned CD-ROM product that would have listed demographic data on 80 million households. State governments have filed suit against the largest credit firms for allegedly keeping old and inaccurate data in their files. And Congress has been considering a variety of bills that would provide the public with greater protections from external uses of private information. Data privacy is a particularly hot issue in Europe. The European Community has been considering passing very stringent data-protection laws that would severely limit companies' rights to collect and sell personal information.

On a similar note, as more companies set up a competitive intelligence function within their firms, there is increasing attention and awareness of the kinds of information-gathering techniques that could be considered unethical, or even illegal. Recent articles in the popular press have described a number of cases where a company's quest for information on its competitors went too far. Such inappropriate information-gathering activities, which are sometimes termed "industrial espionage," run the gamut from outright theft of documents to wiretapping, looking through trash, and telephoning and questioning competitors using an assumed name and phony purpose.

Hewlett-Packard, among other companies, has developed an ethics policy (called the "Standards of Business Conduct") designed to prevent unethical information-gathering activities. Hewlett-Packard's policy on obtaining competitive information reads as follows:

> Hewlett-Packard [HP] is entitled to keep up with competitive developments and may review all pertinent public information concerning competitive products. However, HP may not even attempt through improper means to acquire a competitor's trade secrets or other proprietary or confidential information including information as to facilities, manufacturing capacity, technical developments or customers. Improper means include industrial espionage, inducing a competitor's personnel to disclose confidential information, or other means that are not open and aboveboard.

Your company may want to consider creating its own ethical guidelines for information-gathering.

7

What Computer Databases Can Do for You

Databases have been around for hundreds of years. Surprised? If so, it's probably because (like many people) you confuse ordinary databases with online databases. It's only the latter that are high-tech and computerized. Ordinary databases are actually nothing more than a collection of information. For example, your Rolodex is a database of the phone numbers of your business contacts. Your phone book is a database of names, addresses, and phone numbers of people who live in your city. Your top file drawer may be a database of correspondence you recently mailed out. So, there's nothing mysterious or futuristic about a database!

But—once you take that ordinary database, put it onto a computer system, and create an "online database," you have indeed taken a giant leap forward. For then you have created a powerful information storage and retrieval system.

Some databases are bibliographic, storing the full text or references to and summaries of articles in periodicals, journals, newspapers, and the like. For example, articles from *The New*

York Times are stored on a database called *Nexis*, distributed by Mead Data Central.

Other databases store an incredible amount of statistical data, such as demographic statistics, econometric data, stock and bond prices, buying power information, and the like. For instance, the *United States Prices Data Bank* (available through Data Resources, Inc.) stores consumer, wholesale, and industrial price indices complied by the Bureau of Labor Statistics. The *Value Line Data Base* (maintained by Arnold Bernhard & Co.) stores financial data on United States firms.

Still other databases keep track of things like foundation grants, research in progress, patents and trademarks, available technology, and government documents. For example, a database called *CIS Index* (produced by Congressional Information Services) covers United States Congress publications, hearings, House and Senate reports, etc.

Some databases specialize in forecasting and allow you to perform correlations and analyses. Some databases include complex econometric models that enable users to measure alternatives through mathematical simulations.

There are now thousands of different computer databases in existence, and the number is growing daily. They include literally millions of items of information readily retrievable by anyone with a computer terminal. The databases are created and maintained by a wide variety of organizations, big and small, public and private. These database "producers" include press organizations like Associated Press and Reuters, public institutions like the National Library of Medicine, specialized technical information producers like Predicasts, and so on. Most of them have only become available since the mid-1970s.

Why Use Online Databases?

Databases can be searched by the use of virtually any computer terminal connected to a modem. Through your computer terminal, you can "dial up" a database directly, or connect to a "host" that provides access to dozens or even hundreds of individual databases.

The process of looking for information in a database is called a "search." To perform a search, you sit at a terminal, dial an online database or host, and select the individual database to be searched. To ask the particular database chosen for specific information, you enter an appropriate set of terms, and, in a matter of seconds, the computer responds with an answer that appears on your screen. You are then usually given the option of printing out the information if you so desire. The typical printout will show either the series of statistics requested or information about published articles on the subject, often including brief abstracts or summaries. Note that while some databases are able to provide only one- to two-paragraph summaries or "abstracts" of original articles, an increasing number of databases can provide the complete original text.

The world of commercially available online information systems is just about twenty-five years old. But it has already dramatically changed the way many leading corporations and sophisticated information users gather data. It has been estimated that in 1965 there were probably fewer than 20 databases available to the public for information retrieval purposes. Today there are more than 5,000.

Why use a computer database? Computer databases provide enormous advantages and benefits in locating information.

❏ MASSIVE SIZE

Online databases are normally kept on huge data storage devices. These can store literally millions of information items, or "records," in online lingo. It would be literally impossible to manually search through this amount of information, but with access to an online database, huge data banks can be scanned in a couple of minutes.

❑ TIMELINESS

When you go to a library to do research, you might consider yourself lucky if the source you find is dated no farther back than a few months. But if you're searching an online database, you're quite likely to utilize information produced sometime this week, yesterday, or even an hour ago. Databases vary in how often they are updated, but some are updated on a daily basis, and a few are updated every fifteen minutes!

❑ EASE OF ACCESS

Remember our discussion of the value of your time? Well, which would you rather do—spend a half day at the library or fifteen minutes on your computer? With a computer, modem, and communications software, you can bring mountains of data to you without going to the mountain yourself. An accomplished librarian's average time for a manual search of the published literature on a subject might be three and a half hours, whereas the same search on a single database can yield better results in five to fifteen minutes. The results will be better because in that space of time the computer can search through millions of items in a consistent manner. (It is important to note that many public libraries—and most college and university libraries—now offer online services.)

❑ KEYWORD SEARCHING

One of the most powerful aspects of online databases is their capacity to be searched via "keywords" in "Boolean logic." What this actually means is this. Say, for example, you need to find out everything you can on the outlook for decaffeinated coffee beans in Switzerland for the year 2000. If you tried to get this information by going to the library, you'd have to first check indices under a single term (e.g., coffee beans) and then wade through piles of articles and reports to try and find any that covered your specific inquiry. But when searching an online database, you can instruct the computer to locate precisely what you need—and only what you need. So, in this example, if you searched an online database of market forecasts, you could instruct the computer to retrieve only those that mention Switzerland, decaffeinated coffee, and the year 2000.

What Types of Databases Are There?

Today there are over 5,000 different databases covering almost as many subjects, ranging from agriculture and architecture to trade names and textile technology. Databases consist of individual items or "records," which consist of different types of information, depending on the nature of the particular database. For example, some database records consist of magazine article abstracts; others list company names and addresses; a different set may include market research studies; and so on. Here's a sampling of what types of databases exist today:

- Abstracts from management publications.
- Aerospace references.
- Banking news.
- The Bible.
- Biotechnology industry news.
- Chemical substance news.
- Company Securities and Exchange Commission filings.
- Computer news.
- Copyrights and trademarks.
- Defense Department contractors.
- Dun & Bradstreet credit reports.
- Environmental data and news.
- European company data.
- Foundation grants.

- Geological information.
- Market research reports.
- Medical news.
- Merger and acquisitions filings.
- New product announcements.
- Pharmaceutical industry news.
- Popular magazine abstracts.
- Psychological studies.
- Public opinion polls.
- Reuters News Service.
- Toxic chemicals and effects.
- Transportation research.
- World patents index.

Now, at this point, you might be saying to yourself, "Okay, databases sound great, but what do they mean for me?" What they mean for you can be summarized in three very simple rules of thumb:

1. Frequently, gaining knowledge means finding out quickly what has been written about an industry, a product, a company, a management technique, an individual, a place—anything. Databases can tell you in minutes what's been published about almost anything.

2. At other times, gaining knowledge means that you need some hard statistics. Databases can be used to retrieve an enormous amount of collected information, ranging from census data to patent data to governmental statistics to financial data to facts on foundation grants.

3. Finally, you may wish to have some fact, publication, or quotation at hand. Many recent databases make entire publications such as encyclopedias, newspapers, directories, and even the Bible available for you to "tap into" for a specific fact or paragraph.

Real Examples

The three rules just discussed suggest the versatility of online databases and their usefulness to you. But rules of thumb aren't necessarily as helpful as real examples. How can online databases really help you? What does the information really look like?

Let's now take a handful of typical business problems and see how they can be solved by searching online databases.

For each of the following problems, we searched appropriate online sources to come up with the needed information. The results of our searches, in printout form, are shown below each problem, and appear exactly as they would on your computer if you were searching yourself.

Generally, we have shown only a small portion of the information retrieved, just to give you a quick idea of what you get. Keep in mind that most of the searches were performed in late 1991. You would get much more up-to-date information if you performed the same searches today.

Also note that searches are normally printed out on paper that is eight and a half inches wide. Here, the printouts have been reduced in size to fit this book. In the original, larger size, the material is easier to read, although we point out that lots of type squeezed anywhere is not highly readable. But that's the format most databases use.

❑ PROBLEM 1: BRAZIL IN A NUTSHELL

You've received a call from the Brazilian Embassy informing you that a major Brazilian industrialist is in the United States and has expressed a special interest in your products. He wants to visit you the day after tomorrow. You know very little about Brazil and, therefore, need a quick rundown of recent economic, political, and social developments in that country. Using databases like *Business International* and the *National Newspaper Index* on Dialog Information Services can make you an expert on these matters in a few minutes time:

Tax and Tariff Breaks Lower Cost of Investment in Brazilian Industry
COUNTRY: Brazil
JOURNAL: Business Latin America - July 1, 1991
WORD COUNT: 632

LEAD PARAGRAPH:
Tax breaks, import liberalization and relaxation of restrictive rules on
computer technology are lowering the cost of investment in Brazil. The
Brazilian capital-goods industry faces new competition from imports, but
expects the changes to eventually help reverse a downturn that began more
than 10 years ago.

The latest development benefiting capital goods is a bill, first proposed
under the January "Program for Industrial Competitiveness" and recently
signed into law, that lifts until March 1993 a 5-8% excise tax known as by
the Tax on Industrial Production (IPI) on machinery and equipment. The same
law institutes 100% depreciation in three years rather than the usual 10.

Economic Woes: Is the Worst Over?
COUNTRY: Brazil
JOURNAL: Business Latin America - June 24, 1991
WORD COUNT: 644

LEAD PARAGRAPH:
Strong second-quarter sales and production figures in Brazil are leading
some businesspeople to believe a harsh recession, dating from early 1990,
has ended. Executives express new confidence in the Fernando Collor de
Mello administration, following the overhaul of the economic policy team in
March. Still, price controls, double-digit monthly inflation and many other
problems remain on the near-term horizon; most firms expect losses or
marginal profits in 1991.

The most recent national industrial production figures, those for April,
reveal the highest level of economic activity in Brazil since President
Collor took office in March 1990. April industrial production increased by
13.4% over March and 36.2% over April 1990. Sectoral indicators confirm the
growth trend and show it extending into May and June. For example:
COMPANY: Eletropaulo, Metal Leve, Price Waterhouse

Economic environment
COUNTRY: Brazil
JOURNAL: Financing Foreign Operations - May 1991
WORD COUNT: 1366

LEAD PARAGRAPH:
Though the government is selectively relaxing the price ''truce'' (i.e.,
freeze) that it imposed when it launched Plano Collor II on Jan. 31, 1991,
it will have to continue monitoring the economy closely to avert a
resurgence of hyperinflation. While officials in the Economy Ministry hope
to restrain the monthly increase in inflation to the single-digit range
throughout the balance of the year, many analysts regard the prospects of
accomplishing this goal as unrealistic.

In the face of mounting pressures for price adjustments and wage increases,
inflation is expected to hover in the 7-10% range during the next few
months. It will most likely then climb up into the high teens and low 20s
during the third and fourth quarters of 1991, when the Central Bank starts
releasing (in 12 monthly installments) the cruzeiro equivalent of some $26
billion that have remained in blocked accounts since the implementation of
Plano Collor I in mid-March of 1990.

Copyright (c) 1991 Business International Corp

```
11154735   DIALOG File 111:   NATIONAL NEWSPAPER INDEX
To save its economy, Brazil plans to amend constitution.
 New York Times   v140 col 3  p24(N)  p42(L) August 24, 1991
 SOURCE FILE: NNI File 111
 EDITION: Sat   9 col in
 CODEN: NYTIA
 GEOGRAPHIC CODE: SABL
 GEOGRAPHIC LOCATION: Brazil
 STATUTE: Brazil. Constitution---Amendments
 NAMED PEOPLE: Moreira, Marcilio Marques--Economic policy
 DESCRIPTORS:   Brazil--Economic   aspects;   Economic   development--Brazil;
    Inflation (Finance)--Brazil
```

```
11139477   DIALOG File 111:   NATIONAL NEWSPAPER INDEX
Quayle sees   increased opportunities' for U.S. investment in Latin America.
    (Dan Quayle)
Broder, David S.
Washington Post   v114 col 1 pA16 August 11, 1991
 SOURCE FILE: NNI File 111
 EDITION: Sun   26 col in
 GEOGRAPHIC CODE: NNUS; S; NC; NMMX; SABL
 GEOGRAPHIC LOCATION: United States; South America; Central America; Mexico
 NAMED  PEOPLE: Quayle, Dan--Foreign relations; Collor de Mello, Fernando--
    Economic  policy;  Aristide,  Jean-Bertrand--Foreign relations; Menem,
    Carlos Saul--Foreign relations
 DESCRIPTORS:   United States--Relations with Latin America; Latin America--
    Economic  aspects;  Investments,  American--Latin America;  Brazil--
    Economic aspects; Commercial policy--International aspects
```

Note that the two above citations, from the *National Newspaper Index* database, provide just a bibliographic citation, while the three on page 76 provided a short summary, or abstract, of the original. Below is an example from *Nexis*, a full-text database, which actually provides a complete copy of the original article. (We have not reproduced the entire article here, however.)

```
                   LEVEL 1 - 1 OF 12 REPORTS

             Copyright (c) 1991 Business International;
                    Business Latin America

                       October  14, 1991

LENGTH: 869 words

HEADLINE: Policy Failures Threaten the Presidency

   BODY:
      Institutional weaknesses and Fernando Collor's inability to lead effectively
in a personalistic political system are undermining  Brazil's  administration.
Programs that have advanced elsewhere in Latin America are stalled in  Brazil,
making it the only major economy in the region not showing signs of
stabilization. As a result, debate is heating up over a change in the country's
form of government.

Unlike the presidents of Mexico and Argentina, Collor never had institutional or
party backing for his reforms. He ran for president in 1989 as a political
```

outsider and remained defensive of his independent position during his first year in office. This approach has failed, however, and his appeals for support from organized sectors of society are now falling on deaf ears. Consequently, little progress has been made on his major initiatives, which include:

Privatization. The lack of clear authority for the use of debt paper in the Usiminas steel privatization led to judicial challenges that halted the September auction. The administration still expects to carry out the sale, but the October 15 date for a second attempt has already been abandoned.

Intellectual property. Leftist members of Congress have blocked a procedural move to ease the passage of intellectual property legislation backed by Collor and long awaited by foreign companies.

Constitutional amendments. Despite several rounds of talks with congressional leaders to eliminate its most polemic points, a package of constitutional reforms--designed to enable fiscal adjustment and open the economy to competition--is given poor odds of passage.

Schools program. Politicians oppose a national plan to build schools, seeing it as Collor's attempt to co-opt leftist Rio de Janeiro Governor Leonel Brizola.

Tax reform. A sweeping tax simplification plan has deteriorated into a simple tax increase proposal with lukewarm support. Leaders of the Brazilian Democratic Movement Party (PMDB), the largest in Congress, will support a tax hike only if given more control over the funds.

Regional integration. Brazil is the only signatory of the Southern Cone Common Market (Mercosur) accord that has failed to ratify the treaty. More immediate concerns have kept the issue off the Senate agenda. Argentine business leaders are now publicly questioning Mercosur's future.

Desperately seeking support

Collor's most important congressional backing has come from the Liberal Front Party (PFL), a large bloc of traditional conservatives associated with

---

❑ PROBLEM 2: DEMOGRAPHICS TO GO

Now you're working for a consumer products company, planning the expansion of Elegant Frozen Dinners, a line of gourmet frozen meals. It's been selling well in the East, and the time has come to expand. You're thinking of test-marketing in a couple of supermarkets in Phoenix, and you need a quick look at the demographics of the population living near those supermarkets. As you can see by the sample printout that follows, you can get quite a comprehensive socioeconomic profile of the Phoenix metropolitan area from a demographic database called *MAX*. Elegant's best success has been in households with incomes exceeding $30,000 and among young couples living in the suburbs. This information is broken down for the more than 2.1 million Phoenix residents.

The demographic data seems to indicate there should be good acceptance of this product line in Phoenix. Even more detailed information is available from the database, should you require it. Some organizations can even print out customized data maps, pinpointing specific consumer characteristics on a block-by-block basis.

PHOENIX MSA

Trend Information (with Household Wealth Distribution)

	1970 Census	1980 Census	% Chg 70-80	1991 (Est.)	% Chg 80-91	1996 (Proj.)	% Chg 91-96
Population	968488	1509052	55.8	2183438	44.7	2488781	14.0
Households	302985	544759	79.8	837848	53.8	985110	17.6
Families		397610		585844	47.3	674891	15.2
Housing Units		596049		966546	62.2	1131933	17.1
Household Size	3.14*	2.73	-13.0	2.57	-6.1	2.49	-3.1
Group Quarters		20556		34180	66.3	39502	15.6

	1969 (Census)	1979 (Census)	% Chg 69-79	1991 (Est.)	% Chg 79-91	1996 (Proj.)	% Chg 91-96
Agg. Income($MM)	3114.7	11642.3	273.8	34061.6	192.6	49593.9	45.6
Per Capita ($)	3216	7715	139.9	15600	102.2	19927	27.7
Average HH ($)	10194	21200	108.0	40333	90.3	49962	23.9
Median HH ($)	9082·	17737	95.3	34036	91.9	42042	23.5
Average HH Wealth ($)				112722		140538	
Median HH Wealth ($)				57605		76756	

Household Income	1980 Count	'80 %	1991 Count	'91 %	1996 Count	'96 %
Less than $ 7,500	94471	17.3	60738	7.2	50963	5.2
$ 7,500-$ 9,999	43210	7.9	28926	3.5	30501	3.1
$ 10,000-$ 14,999	88001	16.2	65062	7.8	59683	6.1
$ 15,000-$ 19,999	80451	14.8	72537	8.7	65010	6.6
$ 20,000-$ 24,999	71547	13.1	72730	8.7	69077	7.0
$ 25,000-$ 29,999	53758	9.9	66697	8.0	70628	7.2
$ 30,000-$ 34,999	37807	6.9	64711	7.7	63657	6.5
$ 35,000-$ 39,999	24215	4.4	60345	7.2	58946	6.0
$ 40,000-$ t9%999	25056	4.6	106932	12.8	117948	12.0
$ 50,000-$ 74,999	17618	3.2	152692	18.2	200770	20.4
$ 75,000-$ 99,999	4764	0.9	48107	5.7	115620	11.7
$100,000-$149,999	2635	0.5	26341	3.1	54063	5.5
$150,000-$199,999	685	0.1	6432	0.8	17223	1.7
$200,000-$249,999	256	0.0	2484	0.3	4654	0.5
$250,000-$499,999	247	0.0	2681	0.3	4800	0.5
$500,000 and over	38	0.0	433	0.1	1567	0.2

Household Wealth		1991 Count	'91 %	1996 Count	'96 %
Less than $ 0		60798	7.3	59224	6.0
$ 0-$ 4,999		94568	11.3	86293	8.8
$ 5,000-$ 9,999		42408	5.1	42056	4.3
$ 10,000-$ 24,999		86965	10.4	86450	8.8
$ 25,000-$ 49,999		109568	13.1	117399	11.9
$ 50,000-$ 99,999		161843	19.3	188988	19.2
$100,000-$249,999		186490	22.3	247853	25.2
$250,000-$499,999		68501	8.2	110400	11.2
$500,000 and over		26707	3.2	46447	4.7

*1970 Household size is an estimate based on 1970 census data. Data on income and wealth are expressed in "current" dollars for each respective year. 1991 estimates and 1996 projections produced by National Planning Data Corp.

PRISM CLUSTER/PHOENIX

Max Area Evaluation System
1-800-234-5629   23-OCT-91

Study Area Summary

1991 PRIZM Cluster Report

		-----PRIZM Cluster---------	'91 Population		'91 Households		US Household Base	Ratio
Group	No.	Name	Number	Pct.	Number	Pct.	Pct.	Index
T1	1	God's Country	27515	1.3	10450	1.2	3.0	40.0
S4	2	Rank & File	12327	0.6	4879	0.6	1.3	46.2
U2	3	New Melting Pot	0	0.0	0	0.0	0.9	0.0
U3	4	Heavy Industry	41363	1.9	14384	1.7	2.5	68.0
S1	5	Furs & Station Wagon	120702	5.5	44816	5.3	3.6	147.2
R2	6	Hard Scrabble	8151	0.4	2344	0.3	1.4	21.4
S2	7	Pools & Patios	110317	5.1	45903	5.5	3.3	166.7
S1	8	Money & Brains	26822	1.2	12683	1.5	0.9	166.7
U3	9	Hispanic Mix	80277	3.7	22313	2.7	1.7	158.8
R2	10	Back-Country Folks	5962	0.3	1868	0.2	3.4	5.9
U3	11	Downtown Dixie-Style	6678	0.3	2006	0.2	3.1	6.5
T1	12	Towns & Gowns	4328	0.2	938	0.1	1.5	6.7
T3	13	Norma Rae-Ville	30151	1.4	8106	1.0	2.3	43.5
U2	14	Emergent Minorities	4851	0.2	1462	0.2	1.6	12.5
R2	15	Tobacco Roads	0	0.0	0	0.0	1.2	0.0
T2	16	Middle America	52033	2.4	19164	2.3	3.2	71.9
T1	17	New Homesteaders	130244	6.0	48390	5.8	4.6	126.1
T3	18	Smalltown Downtown	45395	2.1	20882	2.5	2.3	108.7
R1	19	Shotguns & Pickups	4218	0.2	952	0.1	1.8	5.6
S2	20	Young Influentials	43534	2.0	19736	2.4	3.0	80.0
U1	21	Urban Gold Coast	0	0.0	0	0.0	0.5	0.0
T3	22	Mines & Mills	17135	0.8	5789	0.7	3.0	23.3
U1	23	New Beginnings	204625	9.4	93995	11.2	4.2	266.7
S3	24	Young Suburbia	319342	14.6	109231	13.0	6.0	216.7
S2	25	Two more Rungs	4250	0.2	2184	0.3	0.7	42.9
U2	26	Single City Blues	109180	5.0	47586	5.7	3.3	172.7
S4	27	Levittown, U.S.A.	33585	1.5	13737	1.6	2.9	55.2
S1	28	Blue Blood Estates	22040	1.0	8387	1.0	1.1	90.9
T2	29	Coalburg & Corntown	324	0.0	116	0.0	2.0	0.0
S3	30	Blue-Chip Blues	338257	15.5	112380	13.4	6.2	216.1
U1	31	Black Enterprise	4083	0.2	1632	0.2	0.7	28.6
U3	32	Public Assistance	10773	0.5	3462	0.4	2.7	14.8
T3	33	Golden Ponds	87763	4.0	37441	4.5	5.0	90.0
R1	34	Agri-Business	25484	1.2	7835	0.9	2.1	42.9
R1	35	Grain Belt	3810	0.2	1080	0.1	1.2	8.3
U2	36	Old Yankee Rows	11089	0.5	4661	0.6	1.5	40.0
U1	37	Bohemian Mix	2167	0.1	616	0.1	1.1	9.1
R2	38	Share Croppers	14123	0.6	4160	0.5	3.9	12.8
S4	39	Gray Power	176893	8.1	89469	10.7	3.0	356.7
T2	40	Blue-Collar Nursery	42385	1.9	12810	1.5	2.3	65.2
XX	41	Not Assigned	1262	0.1	1	0.0		

❑ PROBLEM 3: CAMCORDER FUTURES

Perhaps you need to know the outlook for VHS camcorder sales
and want some statistics and analyses to determine growth
rates and market shares in this industry. A quick search of the
PROMPT database produced by Predicasts will yield numer-
ous items on the subject. Here are just four:

Appliance   September, 1991   p. 59
ISSN: 0003-6781

9/7/9
03199476
COMPACT CAMCORDERS HOLD LEAD

Compact camcorders continued to hold more than 2-to-1 lead over full-size in May, according to latest EIA figures, but not quite maintaining 70.5% record established in April (TVD May 20 p14). Results.in May showed 69.1% of camcorders sold to dealers were compacts (8mm and VHS-C) and 30.9% were full-size.

Of 216,884 sold in May (TVD June 10 p13), 149,882 were compact, 67,002 full-size. In May 1990, full-size led compacts, 59.8% to 40.2%. For 1991's first 5 months, compacts totaled 531,596 (51.3% of total), full-size 313,295 (37.1%).

Inventories at end of May followed same pattern as sales, compacts representing 58.2%, full-size 31.8%. Total 408,000 in inventory at factory plus distributor level represented about 6.5 weeks' supply. EIA doesn't break out 8mm vs. VHS-C formats.

Laserdisc player (LDP) sales plummeted in May to lowest figure of 5 months reported so far by EIA. May figure in EIA's new series on LDP sales to dealers (TVD June 3 p11) was 8,429, compared with 11,511 in April, 15,276 in March and 11,085 in Feb., raising Feb.-May sales to 46,301. EIA put 1990 sales at 168,000.

THIS IS THE FULL TEXT: Copyright 1991 WARREN PUBLISHING, INC.
WORD COUNT: 179

Consumer Electronics   June 24, 1991   p. N/A
ISSN: 0497-1515
Camcorders

A ray of sunshine fell on the camcorder category, where growth was recorded in both unit sales to dealers and factory dollars. According to EIA/CEG estimates, unit sales grew nearly 30 percent to $2.95 million in 1990. Factory dollar volume jumped 9.2 percent to $2.16 million. According to many industry estimates, the format war between 8mm, VHS-C and full-size VHS is being won by the combined sales of the compact formats. The top format now looks to be 8mm, but no one is willing to sell the other two formats short as yet. Several more years of growth are predicted for the category.

Article includes camcorder sales in 1990 and 1989 and channels of distribution by % share in 1989.

THIS IS AN EXCERPT: Copyright 1991 Capital Cities Media Inc.
FULL TEXT AVAILABLE IN FORMAT 9
WORD COUNT: 140

HFD   March 11, 1991   p. 49
ISSN: 0162-9158

POPULARITY GROWS, 8MM SHOWS TECHNOLOGICAL GROWTH POTENTIAL

According to the 8mm Video Council (New York, NY), 8mm now accounts for 66% of all camcorder use. A survey conducted for the council by an independent market reach firm also found that 60% of non-camcorder owners were considering buying 8mm units. And the technological future looks bright for the format. Aiwa, Canon and others have made sure that 8mm digital audio is comparable to other advanced audio formats, and Hitachi has unveiled a prototype that allows an 8mm camcorder to record digital video still images as well. As digital technology develops, one 8mm unit will be able to record both moving and still images. (8mm Video Council, 800/843-8645; 212/682-6300 in N.Y.)

THIS IS THE FULL TEXT: Copyright 1991 by Vidmar Communications, Inc.
WORD COUNT: 112

```
Optical & Magnetic Report    August, 1991   p. N/A
ISSN: 1047-5117

Consumer Electronics: Camcorders

US camcorders market share, 1990

(% of total shipments)

Sony                                 18
Thomson                              18
Matsushita (Panasonic, Quasar)       14
Sharp                                 9
JVC                                   8
NAP                                   6
Canon                                 4
Hitachi                               3
Others                               20

Total shipments, 000 units         2950
```

Appliance, September, 1991

You can see from the examples above that the *PROMPT* database provides various types of information formats. These include abstracts, excerpts (which are similar to abstracts, but are word-for-word extractions from the beginning of an article, as well as some full text), and charts.

It's worth noting here that Predicasts has created a very sophisticated method for identifying and searching for information on specific industries and products. The firm uses a hierarchical numerical code that can be used to identify both broad and narrow industries and products. For example, the following are Predicasts' codes for a series of products falling under the broad heading of "machinery":

Machinery except electric= 35
Office and Computing Machines= 357
Computer Auxiliary Equipment= 35732
Special Purpose Terminals= 357328
Automatic Teller Machines= 3573282

By using these cascading codes, you can pinpoint precisely what industry and product you need information about, and then instruct the database to locate articles and reports covering just those specified numbers.

This coding system is similar to the Standard Industrial Classification (SIC) code system implemented by the government. It's important that all businesses understand SIC codes and their uses. Every industry is assigned a specific hierarchical SIC number, which is based on a company's primary business activities. The first two digits correspond to a major industry group, and the following digits further specify industry subgroups. Although the SIC code system was originally created by the government for classifying businesses and taking a census, the codes have been widely adopted by non-government information sources, and many major databases index companies and products with SIC codes as well. That's why knowing the SIC system is so important. Predicasts, however, has done even better than the SIC code system by creating a proprietary numbering system that includes even longer strings of industry codes. This way, users can pinpoint specific information needs even more precisely.

To order the guide to the SIC coding system, write to:

Standard Industrial Classification Manual
Superintendent of Documents
United States Government Printing Office
Washington, DC 20402

The manual lists each SIC number along with the industry it belongs to.

❏ PROBLEM 4: QUICK COMPANY COMPOSITES

An investment portfolio you're evaluating includes Dell Computer Corporation. Since you've learned about Dell's rapid rise in the computer industry, a number of questions occur to you. What are Dell's subsidiaries? What is the company's current financial position? Has it recently filed an 8-K, and how can you obtain a copy? What have been the trends in its stock share prices?

A number of databases can answer all or part of these questions; the databases we've used here are *Disclosure*, the *Tradeline* portion of *Dow Jones News Retrieval*, and *SEC Online*.

The illustration below provides balance sheet information.

BALANCE SHEET ANNUAL ASSETS ($000s)			
Fiscal Year Ending	02/03/91	02/02/90	01/27/89
Cash	36,627	NA	2,631
Marketable Securities	NA	NA	NA
Receivables	89,699	60,042	36,360
Inventories	88,462	68,246	103,999
Raw Materials	65,951	34,968	72,303
Work in Progress	20,539	7,542	17,359
Finished Goods	1,972	25,736	14,337
Notes Receivable	NA	NA	NA
Other Current Assets	21,480	14,228	6,439
Total Current Assets	236,268	142,516	149,429
Gross Property, Plant & Eq	26,483	26,170	14,854
Accumulated Depreciation	NA	NA	NA
Net Property, Plant & Eq	26,483	26,170	14,854
Investment & Adv to Subs	NA	NA	NA
Other Non-Current Assets	NA	NA	NA
Deferred Charges (Asset)	NA	NA	NA
Intangibles	NA	NA	NA
Deposits & Other Assets	1,471	3,088	2,749
Total Assets	264,222	171,774	167,032

Income statements are available for the last five years, as listed below. (A cash flow statement and key annual financial ratios are not illustrated here, but are also available.)

ANNUAL INCOME STATEMENT ($000s)			
Fiscal Year Ending	02/03/91	02/02/90	01/27/89
Net Sales	546,235	388,558	257,810
Cost of Goods	364,183	277,826	176,693
Gross Profit	182,052	110,732	81,117
R&D Expenditures	22,444	16,877	7,097
Sell, General & Admin Exp	114,160	80,929	51,198
Income Before Depr & Amort	45,448	12,926	22,822
Depreciation & Amort	NA	NA	NA
Non-Operating Income	-346	-1,292	-370
Interest Expense	1,530	3,364	1,289
Income Before Taxes	43,572	8,270	21,163
Provision for Income Taxes	16,340	3,156	6,735
Minority Interest Income	NA	NA	NA
Investment Gains	NA	NA	NA
Other Income	NA	NA	NA
Net Income Before Ex Items	27,232	5,114	14,428
Ex Items & Discontinued Op	NA	NA	NA
Net Income	27,232	5,114	14,428
Outst Shares (not in 000s)	19,345,254	18,788,800	18,651,891

```
                        ANNUAL INCOME STATEMENT ($000s)
Fiscal Year Ending           01/31/88        01/31/87
Net Sales                     159,037          69,450
Cost of Goods                 109,012          53,420
Gross Profit                   50,025          16,030
R&D Expenditures                5,502           1,583
Sell, General & Admin Exp      27,289          10,304
Income Before Depr & Amort     17,234           4,143
Depreciation & Amort               NA              NA
Non-Operating Income           -1,242             -12
Interest Expense                  869             265
Income Before Taxes            15,123           3,866
Provision for Income Taxes      5,753           1,705
Minority Interest Income           NA              NA
Investment Gains                   NA              NA
Other Income                       NA              NA
Net Income Before Ex Items      9,370           2,161
Ex Items & Discontinued Op         NA              NA
Net Income                      9,370           2,161
Outst Shares (not in 000s)  11,003,093      11,468,209
```

The final report obtained from *Disclosure* shows a list of reports filed with the Securities and Exchange Commission. The data shows that no 8-K reports were filed recently. (Public companies must file an 8-K to report any significant activities, e.g., a change in ownership, backruptcy filing, etc.)

```
DELL COMPUTER CORP

Disclosure Co No: D321450000

Filings:
    08/04/91    10-Q
    05/13/91    PROXY
    05/13/91    PROXY
    05/05/91    10-Q
    03/28/91    PRSPCT
    03/27/91    SHELF S-1 A03
    03/20/91    SHELF S-1 A02
    02/20/91    REGST S01 A01
    02/20/91    PRSPCT
    02/15/91    REGST S01
    02/03/91    10-K
    02/03/91    10-K A01
    02/03/91    10-K
    02/03/91    ARS
    11/03/90    10-Q
    11/03/90    10-Q A01
    11/03/90    10-Q A02
    08/03/90    10-Q
    05/22/90    PROXY
    05/04/90    10-Q
    02/02/90    10-K
    02/02/90    ARS
```

Tradeline on *Dow Jones News Retrieval* shows an increase in monthly share prices since May 1991, though not a corresponding increase in volume.

```
Last pricing date for this issue is: 10/03/91

24702510   K   DELL     DELL COMPUTER CORP

            Monthly prices  5/01/91 to 10/03/91
```

Month Ending	Months Volume	Months High/Ask	Months Low/Bid	Last Cls/Bid
5/31/91	17156400	26 5/8	20 1/4	24 3/4
6/28/91	11580100	26	21	24 1/2
7/31/91	11574200	30	24 5/8	28 3/4
8/30/91	11097300	35 5/8	28 1/2	32 5/8
9/30/91	11205900	36 1/4	29 1/2	33 3/8
10/03/91*	926900	34	30 1/2	31 1/8

```
            * indicates a partial period
```

Finally, a listing of Dell's subsidiaries was obtained by searching the *SEC Online* database:

```
EXHIBIT 22

SUBSIDIARIES OF DELL

Dell International Incorporated
Incorporated in Delaware
dba PC's Limited
dba System Logic
dba Computer Direct

Dell Corporate Services Corporation
Incorporated in Delaware

Dell USA Corporation
Incorporated in Delaware
dba Dell Computer USA Corporation

Dell Marketing Corporation
Incorporated in Delaware

Dell Field Sales Corporation
Incorporated in Delaware

Dell Direct Sales Corporation
Incorporated in Delaware
```

❏ PROBLEM 5: LET YOUR KEYBOARD DO THE WALKING

You're preparing for a three-day business trip to a client firm in Pleasant Hill, California. Since you'll be negotiating a contract, you'll need on-the-spot, top-quality typing support for contract changes. Time is short and this must be arranged in advance. A search of *Dun & Bradstreet's Electronic Business Directory* yields a few choices in nearby Concord, two of which are reprinted here. (Fictitious companies have been substituted for the actual company names provided by the search.)

1/5/1
CUTTING EDGE BUSINESS CENTER
140 MAIN STREET
CONCORD, CA 94523

TELEPHONE: 415-555-1212

COUNTY: CONTRA COSTA   SMSA: 526 (SAN-FRAN--OAKLAND, CA)
REGION: PACIFIC

INDUSTRY GROUP: BUSINESS SERVICES

PRIMARY SIC:

7338   SECRETARIAL AND COURT REPORTING, NSK
73389903   SECRETARIAL AND TYPING SERVICE

THIS IS A(N):
          CORPORATION
          FIRM
          SINGLE LOCATION
D-U-N-S NUMBER: 11-111-1111
NUMBER OF EMPLOYEES   B (1-4)
COUNTY POPULATION   9 (500,000 AND OVER)

1/5/2
CUTTING EDGE SECRETARIAL SERVICE
140 MAIN STREET
CONCORD, CA 94523

TELEPHONE: 415-555-1212

COUNTY: CONTRA COSTA   SMSA: 526 (SAN-FRAN--OAKLAND, CA)
REGION: PACIFIC

INDUSTRY GROUP: BUSINESS SERVICES

PRIMARY SIC:

7338   SECRETARIAL AND COURT REPORTING, NSK
 73389903   SECRETARIAL AND TYPING SERVICE

THIS IS A(N):
        CORPORATION
        FIRM
        SINGLE LOCATION
D-U-N-S NUMBER: 22-222-2222
NUMBER OF EMPLOYEES   B (1-4)
COUNTY POPULATION   9 (500,000 AND OVER)

Copyright 1992 Dun & Bradstreet, Inc.
All Rights Reserved
Reprinted With Permission

❏ PROBLEM 6: PRODUCT AND INDUSTRY FORECASTS

You're in new business development for a large industrial
corporation that wants to diversify into the communications
field. One area that's been identified for you to investigate is
global opportunities in mobile data equipment. You need to
determine demand for this product for a presentation to top
management within two weeks. You begin with a five-minute
search of the *Findex* database that instantly provides abstracts
for a handful of recent reports. Here are just two:

```
WORLD MOBILE DATA EQUIPMENT AND SERVICES MARKETS
JAN   1991   236 P.   $1695   ONE-TIME
  Publ:   Market   Intelligence   Research   Corp,        Mountain  View,   CA
415-961-9000
  Availability: PUBLISHER
  Report No.: 612-60
  Document Type: MARKET/INDUSTRY STUDY
  The  mobile  data  communications  industry  (as  opposed to  voice
communications)  includes  cellular  radio,  satellite,  and other mobile data
communications.  The  list  of  end users of these technologies is vast, and
the market for  mobile  data  communications  is expected to grow over the
forecast  period  1987-1997 covered in this report. The report segments the
market  by  total market, world region (U.S., Europe, Far East, and rest of
world),  and  individual  technology (cellular, satellite, and other). Each
segment  includes  revenue,  revenue growth rates, market trends and, where
applicable,  trends by geographic region, subscriber or unit/pricing trends,
end-user  trends,  and  the  competitive  outlook.  The  report  discusses
important issues such as digitalization, 1992 Europe, and regulatory trends
in  detail,  and includes a list of major market participants and a chapter
on  market  strategies  successfully employed by these companies. Also
provides profiles on selected companies.
```

```
TELECOMMUNICATIONS FOR EUROPE 1992: THE CEC SOURCES, VOLUME 2
1991    730 P.    $150    ONE-TIME
Publ: IOS Press Inc,    Burke, VA 703-323-5554
Availability: PUBLISHER
    This  source  book  constitutes  the  second in a series of three volumes
covering   the   background   documentation   on   European  telecommunications
regulations as outlined in the famous Green Paper in 1987. The first volume
covered  developments  and  legislation  from 1982 to the end of 1988. This
second  volume covers 1989-1990, including ONP, the opening of services and
terminal equipment markets to competition, the Satellite Green Paper, ISDN,
mobile communications, procurement and standards.
```

Note that these abstracts are derived from "off the shelf" market research reports. These studies are written for sale to the general business community, and are typically much less expensive than individually customized studies. If the information contained in a database abstract is not sufficient, you can then directly contact either the database producer or the report publisher to inquire about buying the full report. Reports typically cost anywhere from $150 to $2,500.

You will probably find that most "off the shelf" studies are quite suitable for your research purposes. Should you determine that you need more customized information, you can then contact a research or survey firm to obtain a price quote.

❏ PROBLEM 7: DETAILS ON A SMALL, PRIVATE FIRM

Say you are a wholesaler of a specialty food item. You have discovered that one region of the country where consumers have the demographics you seek is Rochester, New York. Now you want to find out as much as you can about the supermarket chain operating there. But the chain is small and privately held, and there are no filings or public information. Luckily, there are other sources. One online database, for example, called *Business Dateline,* culls articles about smaller firms from regional business magazines. Another broader newspaper database, *Vu/Text,* does the same for regional general interest newspapers.

6/5/1
0218292 91-41059
Big Ad Campaign Seeks to Promote Wegmans Sodas
Le Beau, Christina
Rochester Business Journal (Rochester, NY, US), v7 n4 s1 p3
PUBL DATE: 910520

TEXT:
   WPOP might prove to be a contemporary hit, but it's not a radio
station.

   It's, Wegmans Pop.

   And it is the center of a marketing campaign costing upwards of
$500,000 -- at least $300,000 more than Wegmans Food Markets Inc. has ever
spent promoting a single product.

   "We want people to consider us right along with Coke and Pepsi," said
Wegmans brand manager Marty Gardner. "We've always had the ability to sell
our (flavored soft drinks) well, but we've been weak in our colas."
   New sweeteners and extracts for all flavors, as well as a new producer,
are hoped to change that. The soft drinks are priced pennies above the old
Wegmans brand, yet lower than industry leaders.

   Wegmans declined to divulge the name of the producer, but the cans
state that the soft drinks are a product of Canada.

               COPYRIGHT: Copyright Rochester Business Journal 1991

Wegmans Fined for Price Violations
Norris, Scott
Rochester Business Journal (Rochester, NY, US), v6 n7 s1 p2
PUBL DATE: 900611
JOURNAL CODE: ROCH
DOC TYPE: Newspaper article
DATELINE: Rochester, NY, US   WORD COUNT: 639

TEXT:
   The state Department of Agriculture and Markets fined Wegmans Food
Markets Inc. more than $5,000 after recent inspections of two area stores.

   The stores, on Mt. Read Boulevard and at Midtown Plaza, were charged
with pricing violations.

   The .Midtown store incurred $2,800 in penalties for 55 unit-pricing
violations among 6,816 products inspected, and $1,000 for 212 item-pricing
violations among 341 products examined.

The two preceding searches, performed on *Business Dateline*, provided a short but full-text account of the news story. The following search, done on the *Vu/Text* database, resulted in another, much longer full-text printout.

THE BUFFALO NEWS
Copyright (c) 1991, The Buffalo News

DATE: MONDAY &Aptember 30, 1991
PAGE: B1   EDITION: CITY
SECTION: LIFESTYLES   LENGTH: Medium
SOURCE: By JANICE OKUN - News Food Editor

WEGMAN HAS FAITH IN COMPUTER PRICING IT'S ITEM PRICING THAT LEADS TO
        ERRORS,   SUPERMARKET CHIEF SAYS

ROBERT B. Wegman says he knows a consumer concern when he sees one.
And the head of the well-known*Wegmans*supermarket chain definitely doesn't
see one in the recent controversy over item pricing.
The dispute is over whether supermarkets must put individual price tags on
nearly every item on their shelves. A state law requiring such tags expired
recently; local governments are trying to take up the slack. Erie County will
decide on the issue next month.
Wegman, 72, chairman and chief executive officer of the 44-store chain, has
led the opposition and remains firm.
"I do not think item pricing is a consumer issue," Wegman insisted last
week during an interview in his luxurious Rochester office.

He believes that marking prices on individual items is unnecessary with
today's improved computer technology; it is an expensive process, he says, and
prone to many errors.
Wegman also said that if item pricing does become law in Erie County it
would be a "turnoff" for him. He would think twice before opening any more
stores in this area.
*Wegmans*will open its sixth store in the Buffalo area in November, near the
Walden Galleria.
A man who knows the food business intimately, Wegman began his career in
the first Rochester*Wegmans*store, a small fruit and vegetable market owned by
his father and uncle.
But he is equally expert when it comes to computers and scanning equipment.
"In a way, I'm responsible for all this," he admitted. Long a leader in the
national supermarket industry, Wegman was chairman of the joint supermarket/
food manufacturer committee that designed the Universal Product Code -- the
series of bars on every package that makes checkout scanning possible.
IBM, in fact, put one of its first scanners in a*Wegmans*store, and the
rest is history.
"These days, so much of our lives depends on our having faith in the
computer," Wegman said.
"You ride in an airplane through fog --
you can't see anything. It's the computer that is doing the flying.

"Now, are you going to tell me that you're going to worry that the price on
the supermarket shelf might not be the same one that is in the computer
checkout?" Wegman asked. "I say, forget it."
Robert Wegman is not afraid to stand up for what he believes. When the
state law was still in effect, he improved shelf tags, re-educated his staff
and then gradually removed item prices on everything in his stores, making no
attempt to hide his actions.
His defense was simple: The item pricing law was a bad law, impossible to
understand or enforce.
As a result, the state attorney general's office issued a court order to
compel*Wegmans'*compliance. It has since been revoked. But the issue of non-
payment of fines --*Wegmans*owes about $14,000, according to a spokesman
-- has yet to be resolved.
"I don't care what people think of me as long as I think what I'm doing is
right," Wegman said.
Without item pricing, he says, he can run a better store and save on labor
costs.

Though his grocery chain is based primarily in upper New York State, with stores in the Buffalo, Rochester, Syracuse, Binghamton and Ithaca areas, *Wegmans*has a national reputation.

The chain has garnered impressive citations for its consumer responsiveness and employee relations from such disparate sources as Fortune and Working Mother magazines. Supermarket News has cited the store's produce and deli departments for excellence.

And the stores, many of them very large, have a loyal consumer base. Wegman says that the high level of consumer service has allowed*Wegmans*to be one of the few chains in the country that successfully runs big stores.

"Consumers trust us," he says. He shows off several recent surveys taken in Buffalo's*Wegmans*stores that indicate item food pricing is not important to customers.

But many consumer advocates disagree.

"The consumer has the right to know the price of every item at the point of decision, at the point of purchase and when he gets it home," says Jeffrey Weinstock, spokesman for the state Consumer Protection Board.

Many shoppers support such item pricing, too. A recent hearing on the proposed Erie County bill sponsored by county legislators Raymond K. Dusza, Thomas J. Mazur and G. Steven Pigeon was well-attended by concerned shoppers. (No food marketing people made an appearance.)

Consumers spoke up about the difficulty of reading shelf tags, especially on the bottom shelf; they said scanners were inaccurate.

Others said they fear that supermarkets will raise prices indiscriminately if they don't have to affix individual tags.

Other Buffalo-area supermarkets, especially the Tops and Bells chains, have followed*Wegmans'*lead in abandoning item pricing.

Dusza and Pigeon said they are receiving a lot of mail in favor of item pricing.

But Wegman says that a supermarket has 3,000 to 5,000 price changes a week per store; it would be incredibly difficult to item-price everything. Expensive, too.

It's hard to put a dollar amount on the money that is saved by not item pricing, he says.

"But in the average store in the country (not necessarily*Wegmans)*it could range from one-half percent to 1 percent of sales. Say you have $1.5 billion sales a year. That is not an insignificant amount of money."

And what happens with the money saved?

"I think we reflected it in our prices," Wegman said. "We have reduced prices already."

Most consumer advocates agree that the shopper has to pay more to have his groceries tagged. The question is how much.

"Let them open their books to us and let us find out. Supermarket operators would have you believe that a family has to pay from $100 to $300 more for groceries per year if they are item priced," says Weinstock.

"But we have figures that show the actual cost is closer to $30 or $40.

"And that small amount would be easily be made up by the savings consumers would realize if they were better able to compare prices from store to store." Many downstate counties including Nassau, Westchester, Putnam and Dutchess have item pricing laws; so does New York City. Other laws are under discussion in Albany and Chautauqua counties.

Because Erie is the fifth-largest county in the state, consumer advocates are watching this state Legislature carefully. They hope that with so many counties passing different laws, the Legislature again will have to consider a law.

Robert Wegman, however, says he thinks the Legislature ought to require easy-to-read shelf tags and accurate scanners instead of individual price tags. His chain has done that already, he points out.

"Let's raise the other stores up and force them to follow our lead," he says.

"Accurate scanners would be very nice," Weinstock agreed. "And we're all in favor of improving shelf tags.

"But it's important that consumers realize these are a separate issue from item pricing.

"Item pricing allows consumers to compare prices -- with what they paid last week or what they paid at another store. It increases price awareness; it makes for smarter shopping," Weinstock said. "Item pricing is a consumer right."

ILLUSTRATION: Supermarket chairman Robert B. Wegman says item pricing is a turnoff.

❏ PROBLEM 8: SALES PROSPECTS

You've been given the task of helping the sales manager of an industrial products company plan the development of sales territories, estimate sales potential in each area, and provide the sales staff with better leads. If the product can be categorized using a four-digit SIC code, your task can be virtually completed in a day.

For example, let's assume your product is sold to companies making glass containers (SIC code number 5231).

Searching a database called *American Business Directory* will quickly tell you that there are 316 such firms. The database will tell you their names, addresses, and phone numbers, as well as the estimated number of employees, sales revenue, and market share for each location. Here are the first five listings for the state of Ohio.

```
 4/9/1
08786904     DIALOG File 531: American Business Directory
BOISE CASCADE CORP
290 CIRCLE FREEWAY DR
CINCINNATI, OH   45246-1206

Telephone: 513-874-1770
County: HAMILTON
MSA: 1640  (CINCINNATI, OHIO-KENTUCKY-INDIANA)

Primary SIC and Yellow Page Product Line(s):
   3221   (GLASS CONTAINERS)
   322198 (GLASS CONTAINERS)

Employees at this location:             40
Estimated location sales($):       6,045,000
Share of market this location:        0.105 %
         for SIC 3221 (GLASS CONTAINERS)

This Location Number: 843162389

Top Executive (This Location): DIER, DAVE / MANAGER


 4/9/2
08786903     DIALOG File 531: American Business Directory
AMERICAN NATIONAL CAN CO
4010 EXECUTIVE PARK DR # 304
CINCINNATI, OH   45241-4011
```

```
Telephone: 513-563-6088
County: HAMILTON
MSA: 1640  (CINCINNATI, OHIO-KENTUCKY-INDIANA)

Primary SIC and Yellow Page Product Line(s):
  3221   (GLASS CONTAINERS)
  322198 (GLASS CONTAINERS)
Secondary SIC(s) and Yellow Page Product Line(s):
  5085   (INDUSTRIAL SUPPLIES)
  508529 (CANS)

Employees at this location:                  8
Estimated location sales($):         2,997,000
Share of market this location:           0.052 %
         for SIC 3221 (GLASS CONTAINERS)
This is a BRANCH. This Location Number: 313744864

The Immediate Parent Company is AMERICAN NATIONAL CAN CO.
   Location Number (Immediate Parent) : 402828875

The  Ultimate Parent Company is HOWMET CORP
     With  82 business locations.
     Location Number: 007528870  Additional Information in File 532

Top Executive (This Location): EATRIDES, MARIAN / MANAGER




 4/9/3
08786900    DIALOG File 531: American Business Directory
ANCHOR HOCKING PACKAGING
PO BOX 2008
LANCASTER, OH  43130-6208

Telephone: 614-687-2395
County: FAIRFIELD
MSA: 1840  (COLUMBUS, OHIO)

Primary SIC and Yellow Page Product Line(s):
  3221   (GLASS CONTAINERS)
  322198 (GLASS CONTAINERS)
Secondary SIC(s) and Yellow Page Product Line(s):
  3429   (HARDWARE NEC)
  342902 (HARDWARE MANUFACTURERS)

Employees at this location:                100
Estimated location sales($):        15,113,000
Share of market this location:           0.263 %
         for SIC 3221 (GLASS CONTAINERS)
This is a SUBSIDIARY. This Location Number: 434610010

The  Ultimate Parent Company is NEWELL COMPANIES
     With  66 business locations.
     Location Number: 007526718  Additional Information in File 532

Top Executive (This Location): ROBINETTE, LARRY / PRESIDENT




 4/9/4
08786899    DIALOG File 531: American Business Directory
ANCHOR HOCKING GLASS INC
519 N PIERCE AVE
LANCASTER, OH  43130-2927
```

```
Telephone: 614-687-2159
County: FAIRFIELD
MSA: 1840  (COLUMBUS, OHIO)

Primary SIC and Yellow Page Product Line(s):
  3221   (GLASS CONTAINERS)
  322198 (GLASS CONTAINERS)

Employees at this location:                      30
Estimated location sales($):              4,534,000
Share of market this location:                0.079 %
         for SIC 3221 (GLASS CONTAINERS)

This Location Number: 434609970

Top Executive (This Location): BERRY, WILLIAM / PRESIDENT


  4/9/5
08786898     DIALOG File 531: American Business Directory
BALL-INCON GLASS PACKAGING
29 TRIANGLE PARK DR
CINCINNATI, OH   45246-3411

Telephone: 513-771-0180
County: HAMILTON
MSA: 1640  (CINCINNATI, OHIO-KENTUCKY-INDIANA)

Primary SIC and Yellow Page Product Line(s):
  3221   (GLASS CONTAINERS)
  322101 (BOTTLES)

Employees at this location:                       3
Estimated location sales($):                453,000
Share of market this location:                0.008 %
         for SIC 3221 (GLASS CONTAINERS)

This is a BRANCH. This Location Number: 140039488

The Immediate Parent Company is BALL-INCON GLASS PKG CORP.
    Location Number (Immediate Parent) : 004713574

The  Ultimate Parent Company is BALL CORP
     With  51 business locations.
     Location Number: 006934376  Additional Information in File 532

Top Executive (This Location): CUNNINGHAM, HAROLD / MANAGER
```

❏ PROBLEM 9: YES OR NO? A MANAGEMENT DECISION

Say you're the owner of a small company and a few of your employees have approached you about working from home on their computers—a working situation that's known as "telecommuting." Before deciding one way or another, you want to read something about the experiences of other companies that have tried it, to find if it worked out and to learn about its impact on the firms.

   A top-notch database that culls thousands of articles on business management is *ABI/Inform*. A quick search turns up scores of items, a few of which are reproduced here.

```
The Advantages of Telecommuting
Young, J. A.
Management    Review v80n7 PP:    19-21 Jul   1991   CODEN:  MRVWDJ  ISSN:
   0025-1895  JRNL CODE: MRV
DOC TYPE: Journal article  LANGUAGE: English   LENGTH: 3 Pages
AVAILABILITY: Fulltext online. Photocopy available from ABI/INFORM 340.00
WORD COUNT: 1221

ABSTRACT:  The    technological    advances  of  the  1980s  in  fiber-optic
telecommunications,   the   fax   machine,  and personal computers have offered
business  the opportunity to change the way it operates and make structural
adjustments   in the workplace. Telecommuting, or working from home with the
aid   of   telecommunication   and   computer-based   technology,   can achieve
important   management   objectives   on a broad scale. It allows employees to
alter   their   lifestyles   and   employers   to   better   manage administrative
overhead.   Real estate values and infrastructure costs are also affected by
telecommuting.   Ultimately,  these factors may help sustain productivity in
the   service   sector.   To   better   implement and manage telecommuting as an
employment   strategy,   corporations should: 1. maintain a system of regular
meetings   and   periodic office visits, and 2. identify who is most suitable
for telecommuting.

DESCRIPTORS: Technological change; Impacts; Advantages; Work at home;
   Workforce planning
CLASSIFICATION CODES: 6100 (CN=Human resource planning); 5400 (CN=Research
   & development)


Users Need to Adopt Telecommuting Plans
Eckerson, Wayne
Network  World  v8n11 PP: 27-28  Mar 18, 1991  ISSN: 0887-7661  JRNL CODE:
NWW
DOC TYPE: Journal article  LANGUAGE: English   LENGTH: 2 Pages
SPECIAL FEATURE: Graphs
AVAILABILITY: Photocopy available from ABI/INFORM 15222.01

ABSTRACT:   Although   few  companies  have  adopted  formal  telecommuting
programs,  network  managers  agree that the number of employees working at
home  will  increase  in  the near future, making it imperative for them to
begin  drafting  a  telecommuting  strategy now. An effective strategy will
bring  together  the  network  tools  and  services  needed  to support the
different  information  and communications needs of work-at-home employees.
According   to   LINK   Resources   Corp.,   there  are  about  4.4  million
telecommuters  in  the  US,  a figure that has grown about 20% a year since
1988. In recent months,  network vendors have unveiled new tools designed to
make  it  easier  for  firms  to support telecommuters. AT&T announced Home
Agent,  which  is  software  for  automatic  call distributors that enables
companies  to  route  incoming  calls  and  data to customer service agents
working  at home. In addition, some carriers now provide switched access to
their  virtual  network  services,  allowing companies to extend their virtual
networks to employees' homes.

GEOGRAPHIC NAMES: US
DESCRIPTORS: Work at home; Communications networks; Strategy; Automatic
   call distribution; Implementations
CLASSIFICATION CODES: 6100 (CN=Human resource planning); 9190 (CN=United
   States); 5250 (CN=Telecommunications systems)
```

Telecommuting: Dialing Up the Remote Office
Gordon, Gil E.
Rural Telecommunications v9n4 PP: 26-30 Fall 1990 ISSN: 0744-2548
JRNL CODE: RTC
DOC TYPE: Journal article LANGUAGE: English LENGTH: 5 Pages
AVAILABILITY: Photocopy available from ABI/INFORM 15868.00

ABSTRACT: Telecommuting is the practice of allowing a portion of the
workforce to spend some time each week working at home or elsewhere
off-site, often linked to the office with a personal computer or terminal.
Typical telecommuting applications include data processing-oriented jobs,
staff professional work, and service-oriented jobs. There are 4 main
reasons for the interest in telecomputing: 1. staffing flexibility, 2.
office space cost reductions, 3. increased productivity, and 4. traffic
congestion and air quality problems. Six considerations are required for
the implementation of telecomputing: 1. choosing the right jobs, 2.
choosing and training the people, 3. training the managers, 4. linking
people to the office, 5. handling the technical details, and 6. studying
relevant legal issues. Telecommuting is not a cure-all for US businesses.
It is simply one more tool, an alternative worth considering to help
companies prosper during the changing, cost-conscious business environment
of the 1990s and beyond.

DESCRIPTORS: Work at home; Telecommunications industry; Microcomputers;
    Characteristics; Implementations; Training
CLASSIFICATION CODES: 8330 (CN=Broadcasting & telecommunications); 6100
    (CN=Human resource planning); 6200 (CN=Training & development)

Telecommuting in America
Goodrich, Jonathan N.
Business Horizons v33n4 PP: 31-37 Jul/Aug 1990 CODEN: BHORAD ISSN:
    0007-6813 JRNL CODE: BHO
DOC TYPE: Journal article LANGUAGE: English LENGTH: 7 Pages
SPECIAL FEATURE: References
AVAILABILITY: Photocopy available from ABI/INFORM 1871.00

ABSTRACT: Telecommuting or teleworking refers primarily to the practice of
working at home while linked to the office or plant through some type of
computer or terminal. Interviews with 525 telecommuters and 50 managers
nationwide revealed that personal and commercial factors have influenced
the growth of telecommuting. The most often mentioned benefits of
telecommuting to the organization are: 1. improved productivity, 2.
improved communication, 3. recruiting advantages, 4. improved employee
retention, 5. more staffing flexibility and cost control, 6. less office
space, 7. improvement in information turnaround, and 8. more computer
literacy. Telework benefits the worker in many ways, and many firms
recognize the telework approach as a strategic marketing and sales
advantage in servicing clients faster and with improved quality. Managers
must select individuals who are suited to working at home and jobs that are
suited for telework. Some unions are opposed to telecommuting because of
the potential for workers, especially disabled persons, to be exploited.

COMPANY NAMES:
E I Dupont De Nemours & Co (DUNS:00-131-5704 TICKER:DD)
Beneficial Finance
Pacific Bell (DUNS:10-340-1618)
NCNB National Bank of North Carolina (DUNS:00-699-6193)
GEOGRAPHIC NAMES: US
DESCRIPTORS: Work at home; Advantages; Roles; Managers; Surveys;
   Manycompanies
CLASSIFICATION CODES: 9190 (CN=United States); 2500 (CN=Organizational
   behavior)

If you take a close look at the records above, you'll notice
that at the bottom of each one is a series of codes. These codes
were created by the database producer to assist searchers in
making better and more precise searches. For example, the
"Descriptor" codes assign a one- to three-word description of
the event or activity being described. So, once you realize that
all articles about telecommuting are indexed with the descriptor "work at home," you can then instruct the database to select
all articles that have been assigned that phrase as a descriptor.
Similarly, a numerical code is used under "Classification
Codes" to identify the type of business activity or activities that
the subject of the article falls under.

There are countless other questions that databases can answer. For example:

Need to find demographic data on a segment of the population? Try *Cendata*, the database of the United States Bureau of
the Census.

Want to read a company's annual reports? Search *PTS
Annual Reports Abstracts*.

Curious to see if the government has published anything of
interest recently? *GPO Monthly Catalog* will describe the latest
reports.

Want to read what the major dailies have written about the
latest political developments? Check the *National Newspaper
Index*.

Need to check some facts on a patent filed by a competitor?
Just go online with *United States Patent Abstracts* or *World Patents
Index (WPI)*.

Like to find out if there are any conferences coming up in your industry? Take a look at *Eventline.*

Want to fill in your upcoming speech with some pithy quotations? Check the *Quotations Database.*

Planning on investing in a new technology, and want to know what the think tanks think of its future? Search *Arthur D. Little/Online.*

Need facts on genetic engineering? Search *Biotechnology Abstracts.*

Trying to find an obscure book published in England? Search *British Books in Print.*

Wondering how the public feels about environmental issues? Find out by searching *Public Opinion Online.*

Looking for a journal on the subject of virtual reality? Check *Ulrich's International Periodicals Directory.*

Trying to find out what Japan is working on these days? Search the *Japan Technology* database.

Want to read press releases issued by companies announcing their new products? Search *PR Newswire* or *Businesswire.*

Trying to dig out the facts behind a news development in the computer industry? Check the *Computer Database.*

And, if you're wondering whether your boss really suffers from a paranoid personality or is merely neurotic, you can check *Mental Health Abstracts.*

Leading Business Databases

Of course, a listing like the one above could be virtually endless. In other words, if you have a question—any question—there's a reasonably good chance that there is an online database available to help you find the answer. The following is a sample of leading business databases, and the kind of information each provides:

- *ABI/Inform.* This database scans 800 primary business publications and provides information on all phases of management and administration, applicable to many types of businesses and industries.

- *Business Dateline.* This database contains the full text of articles from over 180 regional business publications throughout the United States and Canada. Articles cover regional business activities and trends, information about small companies, new start-ups, family-owned and closely-held firms, their products or services, and the executives who run them.

- *Claims/United States Patent Abstracts.* This database contains patents listed in the general, chemical, electrical, and mechanical sections of the *Official Gazette of the United States Patent and Trademark Office.* It offers information from as far back as 1950 for chemical patents, 1963 for electrical and mechanical patents, and 1980 for design patents.

- *Disclosure.* This database provides in-depth financial information on over 12,500 companies. The information is derived from reports filed with the United States Securities and Exchange Commission by publicly-owned firms. Extracts of 10-K and 10-Q financial reports are among those available.

- *Dow Jones News.* This service reports up-to-the-minute news on business and finance worldwide as transmitted through the Dow Jones News Service. It provides coverage as current as thirty seconds and as far back as ninety days. A companion database contains a library of all past articles in the *Wall Street Journal* and *Barron's.*

- *Dun's Market Identifiers.* This database provides detailed information on over 7,000,000 United States public and private companies, including address, product, and financial and marketing information.

- *Investext.* This database is comprised of more than 300,000 full-text company and industry reports and analyses, written by brokers and analysts at 280 investment banks and research firms worldwide. Coverage includes 21,000 companies worldwide and 53 industry groups.

- *Newswire ASAP.* This database provides the complete text and comprehensive indexing of news releases and wire stories from twelve news organizations, including *PR Newswire* (company and organizational press releases), *Kyodo* (Japanese news), *Newsbyte* (computer news), and *Reuters* (international news).

- *Nexis.* This database provides the complete text of news and editiorial material from the Final Late edition of *The New York Times*. It covers issues back through June 1980, and is updated every day.

- *PROMPT.* This database provides abstracts and full-text records from over 1,000 publications around the world. It covers subjects such as market size, shares, and trends, mergers and acquisitions, research and development, new products and technologies, sales and consumption, and much more.

- *Reuter Textline.* This database contains abstracts, citations, and, in most cases, the complete text of articles appearing in about 2,000 of the world's major daily and financial newspapers and journals.

- *Trade and Industry Index.* This database provides current and comprehensive coverage of major trade journals and industry-related periodicals. It offers indexing and selective abstracting for over 300 trade and industry journals, plus selective coverage of information from nearly 1,200 additional publications.

How to Access the Databases

Individual databases are typically made available by database "wholesalers"—usually known as "hosts." Hosts provide access to dozens or even hundreds of individual databases. The following are the names of the major United States-based hosts, along with their particular specialty areas. (For addresses and phone numbers, see Appendix II.)

- *BRS Information Technology*. Broad topic coverage.
- *CompuServe*. Home and consumer; some general business.
- *Dialog Information Services*. Vast resources; business; science and technology.
- *Dow Jones News Retrieval*. Business and financial markets.
- *Mead Data Central*. Full texts of newspapers and journals; extensive business and legal data.
- *NewsNet*. Trade and industry newsletters.
- *Vu/Text*. Regional newspapers.

It's worth noting that there are non-United States hosts, too. One of the most popular is called Data-Star, which provides access to many European databases. You can contact Data-Star at its United States office in Wayne, Pennsylvania, by phoning (800) 221–7754.

There are also hundreds of databases that are not available through a host, but only directly from the database producer itself. Many of these are very specialized and of interest to a very specific audience. You can find out if there are any databases of interest to your organization by checking a copy of the *Directory of Online Databases* or any other database directory you can find at your library.

Where and How You Can Perform a Search

When it comes to performing a search, you have a few options. One is to do the search yourself on your own computer. All you need is a modem and communications software. Then you can "sign up" with one of the online database hosts (or with a database producer directly), learn that vendor's command and search protocols, and get started.

A few words of caution are in order if you plan on doing searches yourself. Conducting good database searches is a skill—and a bit of an art—and if you are not experienced, you might not obtain useful results. For example, if your search is too narrowly focused, you may not get any results; if it's too broad, you will be swamped with too much data. If you are imprecise or do not understand the specific rules of the database you are searching, you can easily get irrelevant and useless information. That's why it is so important to read carefully all the search instructions that the online host provides, call any "help" lines for assistance, and attend training sessions that hosts offer to their users. The time you spend learning these systems is *well* spent, considering the cost of conducting online searches and the importance of getting the right information!

Remember this: computer searching can be costly! Since searching databases typically costs from $50 to over $95 per hour, it's easy to see how expensive searching can become, even if you just do a few short searches every week.

Because conducting computer searches is fairly complex, some businesses choose not to do database searches themselves, but instead hire an expert to do searches for them. Two of the options available are information-gathering firms and "gateway" services.

❏ INFORMATION-GATHERING FIRMS

As discussed in Chapter 4, information-gathering firms are trained in conducting searches. They charge you their direct cost to do the search, as well as a fee (usually an hourly rate). The advantage of this option is that you don't pay any fixed costs or worry about training, and you do not need access to a large number of different databases. Furthermore, most such firms retain highly proficient searchers and usually offer related research services.

You need to be a bit careful when choosing an information-gathering company, as abilities, expertise, and prices vary widely. Ask the firm you are considering these key questions:

- How long have you been performing online searches?
- How many searches have you conducted in my particular area of inquiry?
- Which databases and online vendors will you be using, and why?
- Who will actually conduct the search? What is their background and experience?

The best firms will spend a good deal of time with you before doing the search, asking *you* key questions, such as: What kind of information do you need? Why do you need it? What will you be doing with it? Have you found anything so far? All of these questions assist the searcher in making a more precise search, and increase the odds that he or she will find the information you seek. To find the names and specific services of information-gathering firms, check the *Directory of Fee-Based Information Services*. This book is available from Burwell Enterprises, 3724 FM 1960 West, Suite 214, Houston, TX 77068; (713) 537–9051.

❑ GATEWAY SERVICES

Another option for businesses is using a "gateway" service. If you sign up with a gateway, you use your computer and modem to connect to the gateway's simple step-by-step "menu" system. The menu asks you questions, in plain English, about the type of information you need. Based on your answers, the system automatically decides which databases to search and which search commands to use. Connected to a handful of online hosts, a gateway may have access to many hundreds of databases. The search is then conducted by the gateway, and you are provided with the results.

Gateways are intriguing and potentially useful search alternatives, but again, there are some concerns. The biggest one is that the "intelligence" behind the system, which must select the best database and search statements, is necessarily imperfect and is not as likely to make decisions as well as an expert human searcher. Still, gateways normally work quite well, and can be a lot less expensive than hiring an information professional to do the job. The best-known gateway is called EasyNet, and is provided by a company called Telebase Systems (Bryn Mawr, Pennsylvania). Interestingly, it costs you nothing to sign up and search EasyNet; Telebase prices its service on the basis of how much information is ultimately retrieved from a search. If you find nothing, you don't have to pay!

Which Option Should You Choose?

What's the best option for businesses: doing searches yourself, hiring an expert, or using a gateway? Well, as you might expect, the answer is, "It depends."

If you think you will be doing searches fairly regularly—say six times a month or more—it really would pay to have someone on your staff obtain skills and training in online searching. It can also make sense to do searches in-house if you plan on using just a single specialized database in which you can become very proficient. But if you expect to be an infrequent searcher, or plan on searching many different databases or database hosts, you may want to hire an expert—though it still can't hurt to have someone on your staff who knows at least something about online searches. Many companies use both their own searchers and outside information-gathering firms. They use their own terminals for frequently searched databases, and ask the specialists to search databases not directly accessed or frequently used.

Gateways are useful for cost-conscious firms who don't know much about searching and feel they don't need the "value added" that an expert can lend to the search process. All in all, we think it's best that you have someone on staff who has the training and skills to perform some searches, and that outside resources be used when you are short on time, need special expertise, or need some ongoing type of service (e.g., regular monitoring of an industry or company, etc.).

Potential Pitfalls of Online Databases

So far we've talked mainly about the benefits and power of online databases. But there are some pitfalls and potential drawbacks that need to be discussed as well.

We've already talked about how important it is that the searcher be skilled. This point is worth reiterating—a bad search won't retrieve what you want! So be sure that either you, someone on your staff, or someone you hire knows the ins and outs of online searching. One of the major pitfalls of database searching is assuming that because you came up with something from a computer, you have obtained the best information available.

There are a few other important cautions worth passing along. Once you get "hooked" on doing online searches, it's easy to forget that online databases don't contain *everything*, nor are they necessarily the best choice for every information search. Even though online databases contain enormous amounts of information, there are still mountains of data *not* online. These may include scientific and technical reference books, certain government documents, company financials, specialized trade journals, social science research, and so on.

The temptation is to believe that if it can't be found in an online database, then the information does not exist. A very faulty assumption! It *may* be that the information does not exist, but it may also be that it simply is not on any database. Don't forget that, depending on the question, non-online sources can sometimes still be the fastest, cheapest, and most efficient way to go. Say, for example, you need the populations of the top ten cities in Kenya, and you can't find anything online. How about checking that nice set of encyclopedias sitting on your shelf?

Also, keep in mind when searching databases that when you retrieve article summaries, or "abstracts," there may be some details and facts omitted from the complete article that would have been useful to you!

Another temptation is to assume that online information must be true. Nonsense! Information obtained from an online database is at least as likely to contain errors, omissions, and unreliable data as any "old-fashioned" source like a newspaper or magazine article. Online information is (typically) just ordinary printed data that has been entered onto a computer database. In fact, sometimes that additional step of keying in the data makes it even more likely that there will be errors!

To help insure that the data you obtain is accurate and reliable, you can take some "pro-active" steps. One is to become very proficient yourself at searching the specific databases you utilize most often. As you get intimately familiar with a database, you are more likely to spot errors and problems. You should also strive to get a second opinion—in other words, check a second or third source to confirm the information. Also, make sure you obtain key details on the databases that reflect on their overall reliability and usefulness—make sure you know when the database was last updated, how much of the database was updated, and what time frame it covers (e.g., reports from July 1987 to September 1991, etc.).

If you'd like more information on how to search online databases, we heartily recommend the book *How to Look It Up Online*, by online guru Alfred Glossbrenner, (St. Martin's Press, 1987). It is an enjoyable and practical guide to the do's and don'ts of online searching.

What Does the Future Hold for Online Databases?

The United States Department of Commerce expects the online industry to grow a very impressive 20 percent over the next five years. And it does appear that electronically delivered business information will be among the fastest growing segments of the industry. What this means for business, of course, is that as more and more information is made easily and instantaneously available, there will be increased opportunities for those businesses who search databases to get the data they seek.

There's also expected to be an increasing number of "full-text" databases (these do not just provide excerpts or abstracts of original items, but the complete text). One disadvantage to full-text databases, though, is that searchers have to pore through reams of straight-text printouts.

And, with the globalization of business proceeding at full speed, there are more and more internationally-oriented databases being created and disseminated.

CD-ROMs

Some alternative information-delivery technologies are gaining ground. The best known is the CD-ROM (Compact Disc-Read Only Memory)—a product similar to the audio compact disc (CD), but instead of music, the disc contains data. A single disc is capable of holding up to 250,000 pages of text.

After a slowish start in the early to mid-1980s, CD-ROM technology has finally begun to catch on. CD-ROMs offer certain advantages over online databases; for example, the ability to budget a fixed cost for the purchase of the disc (as opposed to paying an hourly online rate), and the ease of simply switching on the computer at your own convenience to perform a search.

Another advantage to CD-ROMs is that some systems are capable of reproducing the original articles, including all the graphics and other original page layout elements. This makes for much easier reading of the full-text material. For example, UMI/Data Courier sells a CD-ROM system called *Business Periodicals on Disc*, which contains thousands of business articles. Users can search and then print out an identical copy of the original pages—including charts, bold print, design, and all the other original design elements.

Drawbacks to CD-ROMs include the initial investment in a CD-ROM reader, which can cost between $500 and $1,500; the costs of the discs themselves, which typically range from the low hundreds to upper thousands; and the still somewhat limited number of discs available, though this number is increasing very rapidly. In addition, online providers store a much greater amount of information on their mainframe computers, and their databases can be updated much more quickly.

Here is a sample of some of the CD-ROM discs now available:

- *The Art Index.*
- *Chemical Information.*
- *Directory of Addresses and Phone Numbers.*
- *Dun & Bradstreet Million Dollar Directory.*
- *Environmental Abstracts.*
- *The Pesticides Disk.*
- *Standard and Poor's Corporations.*
- *Tax Library.*

Of course, there are many more. (For the names of directories listing current CD-ROMs, see Appendix II.) In fact, new and interesting CD-ROM products are being introduced almost every day now. One recent example is *Business America—ON DISC*, a CD-ROM that contains a database of 10 million businesses that you can search by type of business, geographic location, number of employees, etc. It's a great tool for business-to-business marketing purposes. It's available from a company called American Business Information in Omaha, Nebraska. (Phone 402-593-4500.) This database is also available in a variety of other formats, including lists and directories.

Who is likely to "win" the electronic information contest— CD-ROMs or online databases? Actually, the most likely scenario for the foreseeable future is that both formats coexist comfortably. Online databases are still the best choice for accessing the most time-sensitive information (e.g. news wires, "real time" financial data, daily papers, etc.) and the most massive data banks. CD-ROMs are excellent for easy access to "static" data, e.g., past journal articles, company directories and filings, etc. It's worth noting that vendors of CD-ROMs can and often do send users regular updates, typically on a quarterly or monthly basis. Some vendors are now offering combination products: CD-ROM database discs for accessing archival data, along with an online service hook-up so that customers can obtain the most current information.

900 Phone Numbers

Another competitor, so to speak, to online databases is the 900 phone number. While that exchange has been associated with shady practices and telephone pornography, a legitimate 900-number information industry has exploded at the same time. According to the market research firm Link Resources in New York City, 900-phone number providers are estimated to have generated $690 million in 1990; that number is expected to hit $1 billion by the end of 1991 and then $1.4 billion by 1994.

One example of a very interesting 900 information service is the newly launched *Thomas Register by Fax. Thomas Register* is a well-known national directory of manufacturers, their addresses, and their products. With this system, users dial a 900 phone number, input a credit card number, and then conduct an "information search" by pressing letters on the telephone keypad (to spell out product names, etc.). The system then conducts an automatic search of the *Thomas Register* online, and faxes the output to the customer.

The big advantage to 900 information numbers is that the user doesn't need to know anything about online searching, and doesn't even need a computer. Billing is simple, as users are typically charged on a per-minute basis and the fee is added directly to their phone bill. However, like the gateway services mentioned earlier, 900 phone numbers are still not really suitable for sophisticated searching, and capabilities are still limited. It is expected, though, that other business directories will also soon be available via 900 phone numbers as the technology becomes more refined.

8

A Prescription for Information Paralysis

A peculiar disease afflicts all kinds of people in America. It attacks executives, professionals, and even homemakers with equal impunity. The best doctors rarely diagnose it, certainly cannot cure it, and, in fact, are often afflicted with it themselves.

It's called "information paralysis."

Information paralysis is the inability to proceed from a question to the actual act of beginning to gather the information needed for the answer. Otherwise intelligent people who understand the value of information and have even gone so far as to formulate extremely perceptive questions can do nothing further. Total paralysis strikes. They don't know what to do, where to start, or how to go about it. Fear takes over.

The best cure for information paralysis is to become an expert information specialist who is thoroughly familiar with thousands of sources of information. This book is not designed to help you do that. For that matter, we suspect that you do not want to abandon your present career. Instead, we'll try to provide the second-best cure, which involves two things: first, an understanding of the basic types of information sources that exist; and second, an understanding of the basic categories most information needs fall into.

There are really only four basic types of sources of information: government sources; associations; commercial publishers, services, and sources; and libraries and educational institutions.

Note that one major type of information source, online databases, which fall under "commercial publishers, services, and sources," are not covered in this chapter, since they were covered in detail in Chapter 7.

Government Sources

Governmental agencies are a tremendous source of all types of information. This includes federal, state, and local governments.

❏ FEDERAL GOVERNMENT

The United States government is one of the biggest information-providers in the world. The various divisions and agencies of the Federal Government produce countless books, periodicals, pamphlets, and data sources every year. Topics run the gamut from helpful consumer "how-to" pamphlets to technical scientific briefings to business start-up guides to international political analyses. It would be impossible to describe even in a whole book all of the different information resources published by the Federal Government.

Each major department of the Federal Government contains scores of subagencies and bureaus, each with its own publications and areas of specialization. For example, one of the best sources of business information, the United States Department of Commerce, consists of these smaller agencies and bureaus:

- Bureau of the Census.
- Bureau of Economic Analysis.
- International Trade Administration.

- Minority Business Development Agency.
- National Bureau of Standards.
- National Oceanic and Atmospheric Administration.
- National Technical Information Service.
- Patent and Trademark Office.

Each of these divisions has its own information collection and dissemination operations. This pattern is repeated in most of the other government agencies, e.g., the departments of agriculture, defense, and energy, and bodies like the Securities and Exchange Commission, the Federal Communications Commission, the Food and Drug Administration, and the Environmental Protection Agency.

Many of these agencies, in addition to collecting and disseminating information, also operate full-scale information clearinghouses, such as the National Center for Health Statistics (in the Department of Health and Human Services) or the Office of Educational Research and Improvement (in the Department of Education).

There is a monumental amount of published information emanating from the Federal Government, everything from basic reference books like the *Statistical Abstract of the United States*, published by the Bureau of the Census, to obscure technical manuals on scientific discoveries from federal laboratories. There are basic sources like *County Business Patterns*, which contains statistics on county, state, and overall United States employment, size of reporting business units, and payrolls for fifteen broad industry categories; and *Survey of Current Business*, which is the official source for the Gross National Product figure, among other key statistics. But much of the government's data resources are unpublished as well.

For example, there are countless immigration records—but these are not published in a formal sense; you would have to request them if you wanted them. And some federal information sources do not even exist in printed form. For instance, there are hundreds of expert analysts who work in the Department of State who specialize in studying and analyzing different countries. They do not publish their findings, but can be telephoned and queried by people who have relevant questions.

Another federal information source is the United States Congress. Both the Senate and the House have committees and subcommittees (not to mention task forces and project teams) that collect loads of information, much of which gets published in one form or another. Much of this information is provided by expert witnesses who testify at congressional hearings. For example, if you wanted some inside facts on the 900-phone number industry, a recent hearing on data privacy called on a variety of expert witnesses who provided key insights into the marketing of the telecommunications industry. (For information on how to access this data, see the appendices.)

Another federal source is the court system, which includes the federal and state courts, as well as special courts such as the United States Customs Court, the United States Tax Court, and the United States Court of Claims.

❏ STATE GOVERNMENT

A great deal of useful business information is available from the states. In fact, in recent years, as the Federal Government has shrunk and cut back services, many of the federal agencies' duties and responsibilities have been picked up by the State governments. Consequently, they now collect and disseminate more information.

Each state differs in the precise types of information it makes available, but there are certain similarities. For example, you can normally find a "secretary of state" office that contains a number of records about companies incorporated in that state. An "economic development" (or similarly named) office may have information and statistics about general economic conditions in the state, as would a "licensing bureau" that issues permits for various regulated businesses, such as real estate brokers or pharmacists. One very useful office is that of the "state attorney general," which keeps records on any criminal investigations against companies operating within the state.

Here is a list of the typical types of offices you will find in a State government:

- Aging.
- Agriculture.
- Air Pollution.
- Alcohol and Drug Abuse.
- Arts.
- Banking.
- Civil Rights.
- Consumer Affairs.
- Criminal Justice.
- Disabled Citizens.
- Disaster Preparedness.
- Education.
- Energy.
- Environment.
- Fish and Game.
- Hazardous Materials.
- Health.
- Highways.
- Housing.
- Labor.
- Mental Health.
- Natural Resources.
- Taxation.
- Tourism.
- Transportation.
- Women.

Most states also produce what are known as "state industrial directories," which are valuable listings of manufacturing and other types of companies operating within the state.

❑ LOCAL GOVERNMENTS

Finally, a variety of useful information can be found in county, city, and town offices. For example, county and city clerks keep a wealth of data on births, deaths, marriages, and divorces. They also keep records on property holdings and permits. Specific departments also keep other kinds of records. For example, most localities have a "buildings" division that issues permits for businesses that want to put up a new building. All of these records are normally available for the asking.

This brings us to our next point: how much of this governmental data is available to the public? *The vast majority of records and information collected by the different governmental agencies is available to any individual or business for the asking.* The Freedom of Information Act of 1966 requires federal agencies to provide the public with any identifiable records upon request, unless the information falls into a special exempted category such as national defense or personal data. If you are having trouble obtaining some information you think you legitimately should have, you should file a formal Freedom of Information request (which can be appealed if you are turned down), or contact the Freedom of Information Clearinghouse in Washington, DC, for further assistance.

Associations

A fantastic source for all kinds of information is associations. Today there are tens of thousands of organizations around the country devoted to thousands of different subjects. Types of associations range from the well-known professional ones, like the American Medical Association and the American Booksellers Association, to lesser-known industry organizations like the International Academy of Twirling Teachers and the National Association for Veterinarian Acupuncture, to special-interest business groups like the Valve Manufacturers Association or the World Insulation and Acoustic Congress.

A casual thumbing through the "bible" of associations, Gale Research's *Encyclopedia of Associations*, which lists over 22,000 associations, reveals the incredible scope of these groups. Want to know about the skies? Try the International Society of Planetariums, which has about 400 members. Thinking of getting into raising sheep? Depending on what breed of sheep captures your fancy, you can call any one of the more than 30 different sheep breeder associations. Got a new-age cure for an old ailment? You might want to check with the American Holistic Medical Association.

Associations are great starting points when you're looking for information. Frequently, they have their own libraries and publish statistics and other facts on the industries or activities they represent. Furthermore, they are usually quite cooperative in answering questions because, after all, they exist to promote the interest of their members. Of course, you should keep in mind that their information is not necessarily the most objective.

Commercial Publishers, Services, and Sources

There is an absolute multitude of books, periodicals, directories, indices, guides, statistical compilations, services, and sources that are commercially produced for informational purposes.

❏ REFERENCE PUBLICATIONS

Included in this category are such standard company directories as *Dun & Bradstreet Million Dollar Directory, Standard & Poor's Register,* and *Ward's Business Directory,* all of which provide facts and statistics on larger businesses; indices like *Business Periodicals Index* and *Funk & Scott,* which identify business periodical articles on companies, industries, products, etc.; and countless other guides and statistical compilations.

In fact, there are so many reference guides and directories that there is even a "directory of directories"—*Directories in Print,* published by Gale Research. This guide is actually one of the best places to begin a literature search on a topic, as it covers so many subjects and is so easy to find and use.

❏ PERIODICALS

Just as there is an association for virtually any conceivable topic, so too is there a publication on just about anything, for just about anyone. For example, if you are interested in alternatives to chemicals, you could get a copy of the *Journal of Pesticide Reform*; or if your fancy is flying rodents, there is the *Bat Research News*. Other publications you might browse through include *Diesel Fuel Oils Magazine* or *Hosiery & Underwear*.

Should you want to find a specific magazine or newsletter, there are a few different directories of periodicals you can check. Two of the best-known are the *Gale Directory of Publications* and the *Standard Periodical Directory*. Both are available at most libraries, and both list thousands of special-interest publications.

One other useful aspect of trade publications is that many of them publish special issues that can be valuable information sources. For example, some publish annual "buyer's guide" issues that list names and addresses of manufacturers and products. Other special issues include annual statistical compilations, such as salary surveys or year-end sales statistics. Because these publications are usually supported by advertising, they are generally very inexpensive.

❏ SPECIAL INFORMATION SERVICES

Depending upon the industry or profession and its information needs, there are a host of special services. For example, R.L. Polk & Company and Ward's Reports, Inc. both publish a variety of data on the automotive industry. There are loose-leaf services that will keep you updated weekly, monthly, or even daily in a field of interest. Organizations like the Conference Board and the Research Institute of America (both in New York City) publish a variety of reports on business management, affairs, and other topics. Firms like Arthur D. Little and the Stanford Research Institute produce special reports on industries and markets; these are mailed periodically to members, who pay large annual fees and can call upon the firms for consultation. One of the most well-known information services is Dun & Bradstreet, which, along with its many other activities, issues credit reports that are among the few in-depth sources of information available about privately held companies.

❏ INVESTIGATIVE SERVICES

If you are about to sign a million-dollar deal with someone you met only a few months ago, you obviously need to know with as much certainty as possible the background, credentials, and integrity of that person. But background information on individual executives, information on privately held companies, and other types of information, such as litigation histories, are extremely difficult to obtain. While much of this type of data *is* available in public records and databases if you look hard and long enough, sometimes you may need the service of an expert investigator. There are a number of investigative services throughout the country that do investigative reports on corporations and executives. Among the best known are companies like Bishop's Services Inc. and Kroll Associates in New York City, the Dow Services Group in Boston, and Beltrante & Associates in Washington, DC.

❏ ONLINE DATABASES

As mentioned at the beginning of this chapter, online databases are covered in detail in Chapter 7. You should note, however, that many commercial databases are also available in print, CD-ROM, and other formats. For example, the *F&S Index of Corporations and Industries* (published by Predicasts) is an index that covers company, industry, and product information from thousands of periodicals. It was originally available only in printed form, but is now also an online database.

❏ MARKET RESEARCH AND SURVEY FIRMS

Market research and survey firms are engaged mostly in primary research activities of one sort or another—i.e., they interview people to find out their opinions, preferences, behaviors, and the like. Or they may directly measure, via surveys, things like sales of a particular product or size of an industry. There are three major types of survey techniques:

1. *Consumer Panels*. These are carefully selected groups of individual consumers who periodically report on various aspects of their buying behavior, attitudes, and intentions. National Family Opinion, Inc., is a well-known firm that runs consumer panels. These panels are highly useful when you want, for example, to have a continual measurement of consumer attitudes toward your product.

2. *Syndicated Audits*. In syndicated audits, firms like A.C. Nielsen Company continuously monitor the movement of products through stores by type of product, brand, and even package size. They compile the results and sell them for very high prices. UPC bar-code scanning has added a great new level of detail to the information being captured by these firms, and has made their services even more valuable.

3. *Published Field Interviews*. Typical of this type of firm is the F.W. Dodge Division of McGraw-Hill Information Systems. It collects construction data through hundreds of interviews, supplementing this with other information and publishing thousands of reports each month on building projects.

4. *Consumer Surveys*. Consumer survey firms conduct surveys on either a syndicated or custom basis. Typical of syndicated surveys are the regularly-issued Gallup polls, where the results are offered to many participants. Some firms run what are called "omnibus" surveys, which regularly survey a national probability sample of respondents. Custom surveys, of course, can be done on just about any subject.

Libraries and Educational Institutions

Libraries are, of course, fabulous sources. It is important, though, to distinguish between the various types of libraries. Types of libraries are public, university, and "special" libraries.

The best public libraries are normally those located in larger cities, as these have the most complete reference collections, as well as access to the latest computer-based retrieval technologies. Many libraries make available to their patrons state-of-the-art CD-ROM data retrieval systems that can be used to obtain abstracts of articles published in hundreds of business periodicals, cutting research time significantly. Some of the most popular of these systems are produced by a company called the Information Access Company.

University and college libraries are also excellent resource centers. You will often find that a college or university library offers resources superior to those of a large public library. (This is because public libraries are often strapped for cash, while college libraries are often privately funded.) Many college and university libraries will allow anyone to come in and use their resources, although you won't be allowed to check anything out.

Special libraries are located in businesses or other institutions, such as museums, research institutes, and so forth. While they are not "public" in that they are not funded by tax dollars, many of them allow outside researchers to come in and use their information resources. So, for example, if you were researching the lighting industry, you might try and see if you could use General Electric's corporate library, or that of another firm in the industry.

Often overlooked—but potentially valuable—sources of information are educational institutions and publications. Individual college and university professors are information resources in their areas of expertise, and many universities have set up "faculty databases" that offer specialized professorial knowledge online. Doctoral dissertations can be excellent sources for research on obscure or narrow subjects not covered elsewhere. A computerized compilation of all dissertations can be searched by contacting University Microfilms of Ann Arbor, Michigan.

Related organizations with educational missions can also be worthwhile sources. For example, most museums have a library or information services department—the Smithsonian

Institution in Washington, DC, is a treasure-house of free data. There are directories of non-profit research centers, too: you can check Gale Research's *Research Centers Directory* to find the names of—and contacts for—thousands of different university, government, and non-profit research organizations.

Some Sources of Sources

What we have done so far in this chapter is to give you a feel for some of the major types of sources that you can turn to when you have a question you need answered. We have given you starting points so that you won't be afflicted with information paralysis. Whatever your question, an answer can most likely be found within information stored or disseminated by a government body, an association or group, a library, or a commercial publisher, service, or database.

But which government body? Which service?

For specific listings, you'll need to check a complete source book, the names of which are listed in Appendix I. But if you don't want to read a source book, there is some "quick" assistance available. You can check one of the "sources of sources" guides. These guides are so all-encompassing and so valuable that we will list them here.

What Federal Government body or agency can help me?

Who Knows: A Guide to Washington Experts
Washington Researchers
2612 P Street NW
Washington, DC 20007

Is there an association that can help?

The Encyclopedia of Associations
Gale Research Company
835 Penobscott Building
Detroit, MI 48226

Is there an information service that can help me?

> *Encyclopedia of Information Systems and Services*
> Gale Research Company
> 835 Penobscott Building
> Detroit, MI 48226

> *Information Sources*
> Information Industry Association
> 555 New Jersey Avenue
> Washington, DC 20001

> *Directory of Fee-Based Information Services*
> Burwell Enterprises
> 3724 FM 1960 West
> Suite 214
> Houston, TX 77068

Is there a database that can answer my question?

> *Directory of Online Databases*
> Gale Research Company
> 835 Penobscott Building
> Detroit, MI 48226

Is there a periodical on this subject?

> *The Standard Periodical Directory*
> Oxbridge Communications
> 150 Fifth Avenue
> Suite 236
> New York, NY 10011

> *Gale Directory of Publications*
> Gale Research Company
> 835 Penobscott Building
> Detroit, MI 48226

Is there a market research firm or published study that can help me?

> *International Directory of Marketing*
>   *Research Houses and Services*
> American Marketing Association
> 135 West 50th Street
> New York, NY 10020

> *Findex: The Directory of Market Research Reports,*
>   *Studies, and Surveys*
> Cambridge Information Group
> 7200 Wisconsin Avenue
> Bethesda, MD 20814

> *The Green Book*
> The New York Chapter of the
>   American Marketing Association
> 135 West 50th Street
> New York, NY 10020

Is there a library that can help me?

> *Directory of Special Libraries and Information Centers*
> Gale Research Company
> 835 Penobscott Building
> Detroit, MI 48226

> *American Library Directory*
> R.R. Bowker
> 121 Chanlon Road
> New Providence, NJ 07974

Categories of Information

The second part of our cure for information paralysis is to help you gain an understanding of the different categories of external information.

If you are in business or in a profession, there are certain categories of information that you are likely to need. Indeed, it is inconceivable that you can exist properly without them.

First of all, you need information about your competition—about other companies, organizations, or individuals. You must have information both about individual competitors and about your industry or profession as a whole.

Secondly, you need information about your market, whether it consists of individual consumers or of other organizations and companies.

You need information about the world around you, insofar as it may affect your business or profession. This means that you need to be kept up to date on politics, economics, culture, government, and the environment.

You need to know the best ways to do business. This means you need information on how to manage, organize, and run your business.

You need information on scientific and technological developments. If you're not "in" on the latest, you could be "down and out" shortly.

Finally, you need information on laws, regulations, and other restrictions that may affect the way you do business.

If you can start thinking in terms of categories, you can begin to break down your information needs so that you can properly direct yourself to the right types of sources.

Know Your Competition

In a country as populated as ours, you have competition—whatever field you are in. And most assuredly your success will depend, to some degree, on the amount and quality of information you can glean about your competitors. Whether you are a consultant, or you are running a small hair salon, or you are the president of a multinational corporation, information about your competition is not an elective. Yet the number of people who ignore this is astounding.

Multitudes of executives and professionals lose their jobs

and clients daily. Why is this so? Undoubtedly, it is because they are not performing their functions adequately. One of the keys to performance is having information about your competition. If you are not worried about your competition, chances are that you will lose your job; and if you are self-employed, you will probably lose your business.

What kind of information should you have about your competition? You should know about their:

- Management structure.
- Product lines.
- Sales.
- Financial condition.
- Facilities.
- New products.
- New directions and developments.
- Marketing approaches.

Is this kind of information available? In all likelihood, much of it is. How do you get it? The means vary.

One approach is word of mouth. A funny story illustrates this: Dave and Sam were partners in the ladies' garment business for many years. During one season, they had incredibly bad luck. When they produced satins, organdies were the rage. When they produced nylon, cotton came into vogue. One day Dave came to work so depressed that he bid Sam goodbye and jumped out of their thirty-sixth-floor window. Sam ran to the open window, appalled. As Dave hurtled past the fourteenth floor, he looked into the window of their competitor and yelled up to his partner, "Sam, they're cutting velvets in there!" This is an extreme example of investigating your competition's "new products in development."

Word of mouth, however, is not always possible, nor is it always reliable. But if you start thinking about the different types of sources we described earlier, you can quickly begin to get a grasp of how to proceed.

For example, if your competitor is a publicly held corporation, then it must file information with the government. If that is so, then there must be an agency within the government that compiles or makes available such information. Of course, there is. It's the Securities and Exchange Commission.

If your competitor is a privately held corporation, then it is likely that information about it will be much harder to find. But there are services like Dun & Bradstreet that will provide credit reports; there are published indices that might index anything that has been written about the company; there are local chambers of commerce that might keep data on how the company does business; there are investigative services that will look into the background of the company's principals; and so on.

Similarly, each of the types of sources we covered earlier probably has one or more items of data that can help you put together a complete picture of your competition.

But the primary reason for the necessity and urgency of gathering information about your competition has undoubtedly occurred to you by now, and that is that all of these information-gathering methods are available to your competition as well! If you have competition, it is probably studying you at this very moment.

Know Your Market

All businesses need information on their markets. If you sell your product or service to individual consumers, then you are likely to need information about their habits, their buying patterns, their feelings, and their intentions. In that case, you would direct yourself toward the market research and survey firms that specialize in such things. Or you may want information about the products and services—competitive or related—that such consumers buy. In that case you may direct yourself to syndicated audits, which measure the movement of goods through retail outlets.

If you sell your product or service to businesses or organizations, then, in order to obtain information about your market, you'll have to get information on the industries you serve. You would direct yourself, therefore, to associations and trade periodicals that serve those industries. You might explore what the government knows about them.

Here's a tip on getting information about markets. When you need a quick look at the size of a market, try catalogs of mailing list firms. They are usually free and make for fascinating reading, not to mention the fact that they contain tremendous stores of marketing information. For example, let's assume you've just invented a revolutionary method for the disposal of toxic wastes. You figure it would sell to any company whose manufacturing produces toxins. But how many of them are there? Well, a glance at a mailing list catalog from a firm like Information Marketing Services Inc. in Vienna, Virginia, whose lists are available for rental, would show that there are 30,000 toxic waste generators. Of course, these types of lists may not include *all* of your potential market. But they do include a very important part of it—the part that can be reached by mail.

Another thing to keep in mind is that, generally speaking, the narrower the market, the more unlikely it is that data on it has been collected in a readily available format. The broader the market, the more available the data. Cosmetics would be a broad market; green eye shadow would be a narrow one. It is extremely easy to find studies that have already been published on the cosmetics industry and market. We know of no available complete study on green eye shadow, however.

The World

Every day, every section of your local newspaper has something in it that directly or indirectly affects your business or profession—including the advertisements. The newspaper may not give you a totally realistic picture of what the world is like (you must rely on your best judgment for that), but it does give you an accurate picture of how your community is perceiving the world, and, therefore, how its attitudes and values are being shaped and formed. You need this knowledge desperately for your own success in your business.

Moving further outward, national and international magazines and newspapers can give you both in-depth information and a wider perspective. If your business is to grow, you cannot afford to be provincial in your outlook.

All of these sources inform us about various aspects of the world. Unfortunately, we often need more information about the world than we realize. Fortunately, there are more sources than we can imagine.

Remember the example involving Brazil in the database section of this book? To illustrate how you might suddenly need to be informed about countries far away, assume that you made the deal with the man in Brazil and that you are now an exporter to that country. What's happening in Brazil is now of paramount importance to you—as is what's happening in South America in general. You might now consult the *Nexis* database every month for updates on articles written about Brazil. You'll want to consult the United States Federal Government expert on Brazil. You'll want to know whether there are any private information services that can help. You'll discover a company called Business International Inc. (located in New York City) that specializes in collecting and disseminating information on business activity and economic developments in foreign countries. A new world of information sources and possibilities has opened up for you.

Evaluate Your Management Practices

We have a tendency to do things without considering whether we are doing them right or wrong, whether there is a better way, or how others are doing the same things.

Suppose you are an executive wanting to start a pension plan for your employees. Your first impulse might be to call in a pension expert. But you should think first about reading something on the subject. Why don't you? Lazy? Not necessarily. The answer comes back again to the lack of information consciousness. It is always fine to call in experts, but you yourself should be prepared for meeting with them.

Let's take another example. Suppose you wish to hire a data-processing person. Yours is a small company that is growing quickly. You have bought a mini-computer, and you need someone to run it. How much must you pay a competent data-processing person? You might call a personnel agency and inquire. But the agency's answer is necessarily biased, isn't it? If you were an information-conscious person, you would immediately realize that there must be a regional salary survey of data processors available, and that you could buy that survey.

The same holds true for expenditure norms like advertising, rent, and payroll. Some folks are afraid to discover that they have been managing their businesses or professions poorly for a very long time. But those people lack curiosity and have either discarded this book chapters ago or never purchased it at all.

Government Regulations

Government regulations on any level—town, country, state, or federal—are such an integral part of everyone's business or professional life that ignorance of this informational area can lead to total failure. Regulations are a vital part of your external business environment.

If, for example, you want to manufacture a new detergent and aren't aware that county regulations would automatically ban its production because of one of its chemical ingredients, you are courting disaster.

The one saving grace about this kind of information is that the government distributes published regulations free of charge on request. Your tax dollars pay for its dissemination. But you must take the time to send for it.

You now have the prescription for curing whatever degree of information paralysis you are suffering from. But as with all prescriptions, two more steps are required: you must fill it and then use it. The types and sources of information are all there on the "medicinal" shelves. You have only to reach for them, according to your particular needs.

9

Creating Your Own Information-Gathering System

We stated at the beginning of the book that most people have little idea how to find out what they need to know. Given this, it is not surprising that most people—and the organizations they work in—do not have an effective information-gathering system. How to create one is the subject of this chapter.

Effective information-gathering systems begin with the individual—with you.

Let's say you're the owner of a retail establishment. You "shop" your nearest competitor once every six months to determine his prices and stock. You remind yourself to do this on your calendar. You have started a regular six-month watch; you have installed a system.

Whether you are a single shopkeeper, the owner of a small business, a consultant, or an executive in a large corporation, you must be organized to benefit from information that will further your personal position. You need to be personally aware of your competition. You need the most current journals, books, directories, and other periodicals in your field. You need to make sure you are up to date.

This may seem painfully obvious, yet it is amazing to see how many otherwise sensible people fail to keep themselves informed within their own fields of interest. For example, it is estimated that there are over 400,000 consultants in the United States, but only about 10,000 of them subscribe to the trade periodicals in their individual fields.

Are You Informed?

A simple way to find out is to ask yourself these questions.

Do you belong to the principal trade or professional organization in your field? Do you take time to be active in it?

Do you subscribe to the principal trade or professional magazines in your field? Do you take the time to actually read them?

Do you periodically take the time to check up on key competitors, products, trends, government regulations, or other factors that affect you personally?

Do you at least occasionally glance through your junk mail? (It's amazing what you can learn from it!)

Do you gather information and intelligence at conferences?

Do you regularly find ways to talk to your customers and survey them?

Are you continuously alert to the types of data in your company's computers and how the data could help you?

Are you familiar with your internal information resources (your shelf of books, your company library)?

Do you have a list of outside information suppliers you can call on when necessary?

If you can't answer "yes" to all the above questions, you probably have an inadequate personal information-gathering system. As a result, you probably have inadequate knowledge. Relying on friends, contacts, accountants, lawyers, and advisors is not a substitute for an information-gathering system.

Moving up from the individual to the organization, the information-gathering function becomes more complex, and the systems will vary, depending on the size of your organization. The steps in creating that system, however, are the same.

Whose Responsibility Should Information-Gathering Be?

The first step is to decide under whose direction the principal information-gathering activity will take place. In very small companies or proprietorships, it is usually the president's responsibility, or should be. In larger companies, information-gathering usually falls within the marketing, planning, research and development, or library center, but is often fragmented in many different areas.

It is important to remember that information-gathering and research functions can be organized by product lines, by customer groups, by sales regions, or by corporate functions. For example, product A and product B might each have its own market research department. Or there may be an information system for industrial, consumer, and government markets. Or each regional office of a company may have its own information set-up. In other organizations, the information and research operation is centralized and serves all departments, regardless of product, market, or region.

All too often, the information-gathering function is buried somewhere in "administration," frequently as an adjunct of the data-processing department. This arises because of a confusion between internal and external information. A data-processing department is concerned with keeping track of a company's internal data and should not be responsible for gathering external information. These are two entirely different activities.

This will change somewhat as technologies converge and companies develop top-level information executives with overall responsibility for all the information resources of an organization, both internal and external. But unless your organization has such an "information manager," the gathering of external information should be a function within the departments of those people who need external information the most, i.e., marketing, sales, research, planning, or top management.

Establishing Your Library

Once you have decided who will be responsible for the organization of the information-gathering function, the next step is to establish a library or information center.

In smaller organizations, the library might be nothing more than a shelf or roomful of reference materials. These may include industry handbooks, catalogs, trade magazines, directories that cover your field, and annual reports of your customers, suppliers, and competitors. Typically, the small library should be stocked with such basic information sources as the *Thomas Register, Statistical Abstract of the United States, Business Periodicals Index, Encyclopedia of Associations, F&S Index of Corporations and Industries, Dun & Bradstreet Million Dollar Directory,* plus statistical issues of appropriate trade publications. If your mini-library will not have a full-time librarian, put a manager in charge of maintaining it. Don't expect busy secretaries to do it. This is especially true if you intend to have a computer terminal available for accessing databases.

The next step up is to create your own staffed internal library or information center. It could be small or large and may service anything from a law office to a large industrial complex. Such a library must be staffed by a professional librarian or information manager. This is the individual you will call upon for any and all external information. This is the person who will know how to collect information, how to disseminate it, and how to keep records.

Of course, you must have sufficient information needs to warrant the expense of having your own information center. Staffed by one professional and one assistant or clerical person, such an information center can easily cost $100,000 per year, not including overhead.

How can you tell if you need an information center? You probably do if your company is buying endless duplicate copies of books and magazines, if reference materials are piling up all over, if substantial money is being spent calling all around the United States in search of statistics, if the research being done is less than thorough, or if decisions are being delayed because of lack of information. You *definitely* need one if your employees are leaving you to work for companies with better information resources.

If you do decide to establish an information center, make sure top management is involved in its creation. Set up goals, budgets, space requirements, etc. Hire a fully qualified information professional. If you don't know how to go about this, contact a consultant or the Special Libraries Association in Washington, DC. Make sure the individual you hire is familiar with online and CD-ROM databases and their possibilities. You want a library that will lead you forward into the twenty-first century.

Using an Information Broker

Unfortunately, the vast majority of organizations are simply too small to be able to afford even a small in-house library. Even companies with information centers often find their resources too limited or their staff too overburdened. Furthermore, with the amount of available information increasing, the time required to find what you need is becoming more and more costly. So whether large or small, with libraries or without, many organizations are looking for information assistance.

This is where the information-gathering business comes in. These organizations, which are relatively new and are still evolving, gather information for a fee. They go by a variety of names, including "information broker," "information retailer," "fee-based information service," "information consultant," and "information retrieval service." The extent of the services of information-gathering businesses varies greatly, depending on size, particular expertise, and other factors. While the smallest and most basic firms are often limited to performing online database searching and/or document retrieval services, the larger and more capable firms usually offer the following types of services:

- Access to readily available information in their own extensive, up-to-date libraries. The larger services maintain information centers containing far more reference materials than most companies could afford to purchase themselves.

- Access to a staff of highly trained and experienced consultants, researchers, and information specialists who have the expertise to track down the information you need in a rapid, cost-effective way.

- Access to a wide variety of computer databases, database vendors, and CD-ROMs, for performing wide-ranging searches on request.

- The ability to translate your questions and problems into realistic information-gathering steps. In effect, they consult with you about your needs.

- The ability to perform in-depth market studies, surveys, field interviews, and other research activities, including monitoring and current-awareness services (where you are regularly kept up to date on specific industries, companies, products, etc., of your choice).

- The ability to retrieve copies of articles, government documents, annual reports, catalogs, product samples, or whatever else you might need.

- The expertise necessary to assist you in developing—and even maintaining—your own library in conjunction with the cost-effective use of outside services.

There are large information-gathering firms offering many services, and there are small outfits consisting of individual freelance researchers. A point to remember about these firms is that many offer a creative, consultative approach to information-gathering, but cost significantly less than traditional consulting firms. The advantage of using an information-gathering service is that all you have to do is ask the question. The firm takes it from there. But when you call such a service, try to make sure that you and they understand clearly what the question is, how extensive a search you need, when you need the results, and in what form.

As previously stated, most information-gathering firms charge between $50 and $150 per hour. Some work on a project basis, others on an hourly basis. Some have retainer agreements, under which they act as your ongoing information service or center, responding to your daily or weekly information needs in addition to larger assignments.

We've tried to describe various possibilities for organizing an information-gathering system. How should you organize yours? It obviously depends upon your requirements, but there are some general guidelines.

If your organization is small and your information needs are infrequent, you should rely mostly on information-gathering firms.

If your organization is small but has frequent needs, you may want to have a small internal library plus access to one or more online vendors (like Dialog) that provide access to many databases. This setup can be supplemented by access to outside suppliers such as information-gathering firms, market research companies, consultants, and the like.

If yours is a large firm with infrequent needs, you should initially do the same as infrequent users. But something may be amiss, because a large organization should need information regularly. Examine and evaluate how information is being obtained by your people. Most large firms really should have at least a small library, if only to centralize needlessly duplicated subscriptions.

10
Putting It All Together

So far, we've gone over how to ask questions. We've discussed the cost and value of information. We've shown you the new information environment. We've given you the prescription for curing information paralysis. We've tried to help you determine what sort of library and services you need. You're beginning to think like an information-conscious person. But if you're like most people, you'll want a test run. You'll want to see how it's all put together in practice.

Since everyone's information needs are different, this is difficult. But we'll take a very common information problem—the need for information on a particular industry—and go through all the steps required to solve it.

The Information Report

Assume you've developed a new type of widget. You need information on the widget industry. Assume further that you need to present this information in the form of a report.

The very first thing you should do is to find out whether anyone else has done a study on the widget industry or on any aspect of it. This would save you the trouble of researching and writing your own report. If no one has, you would then proceed to put a report together yourself by gathering all the information you need.

Your report should include:

- A description of the widget industry.
- A description and analysis of the market for widgets.
- The supplier industry structure, i.e., how the industry is organized.
- A description of the end-users or consumers.
- Factors affecting the industry/market.

Section by section, the following is what your report should cover, along with the information you should include and the questions you should be asking yourself along the way.

❏ THE INDUSTRY

Possible subsections include Introduction, History and Background, Products, Equipment, Technology, Product Applications, Trends in the Industry, and History of New Product Introductions.

The main purpose of this section is to answer a very simple question: What industry are we talking about in this report?

In most cases, this section will cover the following:

- Definition of the industry.
- History of the industry.
- Products and/or product groups that make up the industry.
- Detailed product descriptions.
- What the products are used for.
- How the products are made.
- Impact of technological developments.

- Anything special or unusual about the industry that is key to understanding it (e.g., patent expirations, profit margins, tax or tariff policies, government regulations).

Depending upon the industry, some of the items above may require full subsections. In the case of highly technical products or high-technology industries, a discussion of technology might even be contained within another main section of the report.

❑ THE MARKET

Possible subsections include Introduction, Size of the Market, Market by Product Type, Market by End-Use Sector, Sales by Outlet, and Future Trends.

This section should cover the following:

- Size of the overall market in dollars and units.
- Dollar and unit sales by product type.
- Dollar and unit sales by end-use sector.
- Dollar and unit sales by outlet.
- Imports and exports.
- Sales by region or geographic area.

For each case, figures should be given for the past five years, and projections should be given for next year, three years from now, and five years from now. Past actual growth and future projected annual growth rates should be given, with comments on the effects of inflation.

For example, let's assume the widget industry consists of steel, aluminum, and plastic widgets. Each of the three types is made by either a wet or dry process and sold through retailers, mass-merchandisers, and auto supply stores. Major users are few, consisting mostly of local governments and company fleets. A good market study will show, then, the size (in units and dollars) of the overall widget industry, and the breakdown by steel, aluminum, and plastic. A table will show sales of widgets made by wet and dry processes, broken down by steel, aluminum, and plastic, if possible. The percentage of sales of each type by outlet (retailers, mass-merchandisers, and auto supply) should be given, as well as the percentage of each type sold to the end-use market.

Of course, not all markets are ideal for this kind of breakdown, but a good study will strive for maximum breakdown and segmentation.

Figures in dollars should always be identified. Are they dollars at the manufacturer's level, wholesale level, or retail level? Are they constant dollars?

The depth of this section depends on the size, type, and scope of your needs. If your needs are limited, your budget will be, too. So your study will obviously have to rely on published data, which is sometimes good and sometimes poor. In very narrow markets, estimates frequently have to be developed. If estimates have to be developed for most of the market size tables, it is rare that such estimates can be made for past years, so it is better to concentrate on figures for the current year and future years.

Studies performed very early or very late in a year should include estimates. For example, a study done in late 1990 or early 1991 will usually include reliable figures for 1989, but figures may not yet be available for 1990. The study should make sure estimates for 1990 are included, as well as projections for 1991.

This section of your report should make ample use of charts and tables, and the text should summarize the key points in the tables as well as discuss trends and growth rates.

The success of your report will almost always hinge on how well organized and complete this section is. This is especially true for studies requiring estimates (due to the lack of secondary data).

There are some pitfalls to be aware of:

- Domestic consumption of a product is usually measured by manufacturers' shipments, plus imports, less exports. This may not be true in industries where retailers or wholesalers keep very large inventories, or when an impending strike causes an inventory build-up.

- When the market consists largely of imports, it is vital to understand how much the value of the landed import (including duty) is marked up by the importer before he sells it to a wholesaler, distributor, or retailer.
- Secondary sources can be inaccurate or misleading in identifying the size of the market in terms of manufacturer's or retail dollars. One source consistently identifies its figures for certain industries as being "factory shipments" or "factory-level dollars," but close examination reveals that imports are included.
- The definition of product categories in one source may differ. For example, if the United States government had import figures for widgets, the particular widgets included might be different from those included in a magazine's figures for sales of widgets.

❑ SUPPLIER INDUSTRY STRUCTURE

Possible subsections include Introduction, Competition or Companies in the Field, Pricing, Margins and Markups, Distribution Methods, Advertising and Promotion, and Company Profiles.

Once the size of the market has been covered, and you know how much of each product is sold through what outlets and to whom, the next step is to describe the suppliers or manufacturers of the products—who are they, where do they stand in relation to one another, and how do they bring their products to the marketplace?

The most important objective of this section is to identify the leading companies in the field and their respective share of the market. Some historical perspective on their marketshare position should also be provided.

The competitive situation can usually be covered in one of two ways. In the less expensive studies, or for industries dominated by just a few companies, the general description of each company and the marketshare data can usually be covered in one section of the report. In more in-depth studies or in those covering major industries, it is often necessary to augment such a section with a separate section called Company Profiles, in which each company is described in detail.

If there is no company profile section, then the section on the competition should include at least:

- Identification of major and secondary companies in the field.
- Their sales of the product(s) in dollars and, if possible, in units.
- Their current marketshare position and historical trends.
- Major differences between the companies in terms of management, manufacturing processes, marketing methods, etc.
- Major differences in product lines, product types, etc.
- Major competitive trends.

If a company profile section *is* included, it is then possible to go into further detail on each company. Such details may include:

- Names of top management.
- Complete description of product(s) within the industry being covered.
- Dollar sales of company as a whole and for product(s) being covered.
- Profitability of product(s).
- Important parent/subsidiary relationships.
- Manufacturing facilities, methods, and cost factors.
- Availability of resources.
- Labor contracts.
- Company organization, marketing philosophy, and practices.
- Franchises and international operations.
- New products; research and development expenditures.

● Technological advantages or disadvantages.

Structuring a market study is complicated by both the inclusion and exclusion of company profiles. If there are no profiles, the section describing the competitive situation and different companies in the industry can get bogged down in details on each company. If there are profiles, inserting them immediately after a Summary of Competition section can interrupt the flow of the study. Thus, if company profiles are included, it is often wise to include them as an appendix or as a separate section at the end of the report.

Some in-depth reports (especially those done for acquisition purposes) may require even greater depth of information about some or all of the major companies in the field. Such information might include actual operation financial figures, organization charts, locations of plants, biographies of key principals, a bibliography of articles about each company, clippings of the company's advertising, copies of annual reports or 10-K's, etc. Generally, all of these should be included as appendices and not written into the main body of the study.

Of course, the depth of information required on each company will depend mos⁴ly on the depth and cost of the study as a whole.

Whatever the budget, however, a frequent error made in many studies is the failure to include at least a list of the major and secondary competing companies with their correct names and addresses and the brand names of their products. For example, assume a leading product in the widget industry is called Widgetco and that it is distributed in the United States by a company called the American Widget Company. Assume that the American Widget Company only assembles Widgetco, and that the parts are actually made in Germany by the International Widget Company, which happens to own 80 percent of the American Widget Company. All of this information should be made very clear in the study, and the list of producers should include both the American Widget Company and its parent, the International Widget Company.

The section on the supplier industry structure should also cover pricing, distribution methods, and advertising and promotion. Usually, these will make up three different subsections, but that will depend on the individual study.

The subsection on pricing should give a sense of the price ranges of the various product categories. Such a section can also include one of the key areas of a good market study—a detailed discussion of margins and markups. What is the manufacturer's profit margin? How much are the products marked up at each level in the distribution process?

The subsection on distribution should provide a complete description of the methods of distribution used in the industry, including any differences between the methods of the industry leaders. Here's a list of typical items to be covered:

- Description of manufacturer's sales organization: Are the products sold by salespersons? If so, how? How many salespersons? How are territories divided?
- Role of warehouses, if any.
- Roles of wholesalers, jobbers, representatives, agents, importers: Is distribution accomplished mainly through any of these? If so, how? Which major manufacturer uses which? What are the payment terms, commission rates, markups? How much control do manufacturers have over representatives? What is the training of representatives and agents?
- Role of retailers: What are the major types of retail outlets used? What is the role of mass merchandisers, catalogs, showrooms? What are their geographical distribution? What are retailers' expected yearly turnovers? What is the retail markup and profit margin? What are the payment terms? Are there any discounts? Is there price cutting? Are there any co–op advertising allowances? Is there any merchandising?

A very extensive study might include as appendices a table of all products and recent retail prices; a map showing geographical distribution of warehouses, retail outlets, and wholesalers; charts showing sales or distribution organizations; specific documents showing agreements between manufacturers and distributors; etc.

The subsection on advertising and promotion should explain how the industry talks to its end-users. What advertising media are being used, how much is being spent overall, and what are the sales messages being conveyed? Appendix support for this section might include details of advertising expenditure by company for the past several years, tear sheets of actual ads, transcripts of television or radio ads, packaging types, lists of industry periodicals and trade shows, etc.

❑ END-USERS/CONSUMERS

Possible subsections include Introduction, Market Potential and Penetration, Typical End-User, Consumer Demographics, and Consumer Surveys.

The exact title and organization of this section of your report depends, obviously, on whether your widgets are sold to businesses or consumers or both.

While many studies offer a good assessment of the present size of the market in terms of dollar and unit sales of the products, few studies really discuss the potential size of the market and the current penetration. For example, it is valuable to know how many widgets are being sold this year, but it is also valuable to know how many potential users of widgets there are in the marketplace and how many widgets are actually out there being used.

This section should cover the following:

- Who buys the product(s) covered in this study? If businesses, what kind of business? Who is the key individual buyer? If consumers, what are their demographics, characteristics?
- Why is the product purchased or not purchased?
- What are the economic factors involved? (Disposable income, inflation, recession, etc.)

- What are the psychological factors involved in the purchasing decision?
- Where and how do end-users buy the product(s)?
- Any trends in end-users/consumers?

In many cases, the results of published surveys of end-users/consumers are available, and these should obviously be summarized within the text of the report. If an end-user survey was performed expressly for the report, then its results would be very prominently featured and discussed.

Demographic profiles of consumers (especially for products sold in supermarkets) are frequently available.

❏ FACTORS AFFECTING THE INDUSTRY/MARKET

Possible subsections include Government Regulations, World Conditions, New Technology, Strikes, and Embargoes.

This section should cover any factors that influence the industry or market. In most cases, government regulations (their description and impact) will be the major factors discussed.

Getting the Information for Your Report

Once you've outlined the information you need, you now have to go out and find it.

The easiest thing to do would be to hire an information-gathering, research, or consulting firm, or some other information supplier, to find the information for you. But if you'd rather do it yourself, here's a checklist—by no means all-inclusive—of twelve steps to take. Many of these steps can be applied to virtually any information need:

1. As previously mentioned, find out whether anyone has already done a study on the subject. If someone has, and

it contains even some of the information you need, you've saved yourself a lot of money.

2. Perform a five-year retrospective search of published literature (articles, etc.) on widgets, using both computer databases and manual methods. Then, retrieve the full text of all the relevant articles you find referenced or summarized in the databases and indices. Depending on the industry, keep in mind that major overview articles about an industry are occasionally missed if they have appeared in publications that are not indexed or not well indexed.

3. Contact the widget industry association, if there is one, and have it send you whatever information may be relevant. If there is no association, find out whether there are associations in related fields.

4. Obtain data on advertising expenditures by companies making widgets. There are commercial information services that do this (e.g., Leading National Advertisers, Inc., in New York City). The reason this is important is that it will help you identify those companies that are actively advertising their widgets and how much they spend on advertising. This can help define the size of their operations.

5. If your widgets are going to be sold to consumers, you should immediately obtain whatever information may be available from audit firms like A.C. Nielsen Company (Chicago, Illinois). Note that this data will be expensive, but it's worth it.

6. Make sure you get the technical specifications and product descriptions, as well as product catalogues, on competitive widget products. Any patent information can be obtained from the United States government. Catalogs are very useful information sources and can often be obtained simply by calling the individual companies. There are also a variety of commercial information services that have product information.

7. Check Wall Street investment firms to see if they've written reports on either the widget industry or individual companies in the industry. These reports, written for investment advisory purposes, often contain much valuable research information. Many of these firms no longer give these reports away free, but they are generally available from the firms themselves, from distributors like FIND/SVP, or from databases like *Investext*.

8. Get data on imports and exports of widgets from the Department of Commerce.

9. Get all relevant data on the widget industry from the *Census of Manufacturers* and other United States government publications.

10. Get any data on widgets from such sources as *Standard & Poor's Industry Surveys*, annual issues of periodicals, and any other guides and directories. Don't forget to check whether any books have been written on widgets; refer to *Books in Print* (R.R. Bowker.)

11. Order tear sheets of advertisements on widgets. There are services—like Packaged Facts in New York City—that will do this for you. You can also obtain copies of television and radio commercials if necessary.

12. From the foregoing, plus any industry directories or general directories like the *Thomas Register of American Manufacturers*, make a list of all companies in the industry and begin gathering the company data:

    • Annual report, if available. Call the company to get it.
    • Copies of all Securities and Exchange Commission filings, if the company is public.
    • Product catalogs.
    • Literature on the parent/subsidiary relationships.
    • Literature on the major companies in the field.
    • Dun & Bradstreet reports on privately held companies.

- Any available marketshare information on individual companies or manufacturing plants, obtained with the help of services or databases.

While this is by no means an exhaustive list of secondary research techniques, it does cover the basic steps essential to getting information on an industry. Once you have gathered all of this information, you should have a pretty good picture of the widget business.

Primary Research

Now you're ready for primary research, that is, interviews with industry sources, companies, end-users, etc.

From the information gathered, it is usually possible to identify a number of possible experts on the industry. These can be authors of major articles in the trade press, or they can be individuals in associations or people who are quoted frequently in the articles you have gathered. These people can usually be called and interviewed about trends and developments that have not yet been reported.

Next, you should conduct telephone and—where possible—in-person interviews with manufacturers, wholesalers, distributors, and retailers of widgets.

How much will all this cost? How long will it take?

It depends, of course, on the type of industry and market being examined. If an outside firm does the work for you, you can figure that a complete, thorough examination of an industry would require at least two months' time and would cost between $15,000 and $50,000, not including a survey of consumers or end-users. Such a survey might add anywhere from $15,000 to $75,000 to the cost, depending on the size of the respondent sample surveyed, the number of questions asked, the tabulations required, etc.

On the other hand, if you elected to do the same report completely by yourself, it could possibly take you two or three

times as long, not including the survey of consumers or end-
users. Thus, if you earn $50,000 a year and it takes you six
months of full-time work, the cost would be $25,000 of your
time. Of course, this wouldn't include your opportunity cost—
the money you have lost by spending six months on research.

Conclusion

The return on an investment in information is knowledge.

We hope that your return on the investment of reading this book is a higher level of information consciousness.

At this point, you should understand at least the basic steps involved in becoming a better-informed individual—in your business and personal life. You should know how to ask the right kinds of questions, and how to think about ways to find information that may be hard to get.

Ideally, you now have a solid understanding of the sources of information available to you today, how to find and use them, and how to put information to work for your business and career.

Being well informed brings success. Watch how quickly the lights turn green for you at every juncture because of your new state of preparation. Notice how much time you save—and think about the value of that time to you. And ponder the benefits of enlightenment.

Appendix I
Key "Sources of Sources"

The following is a selected listing of some of the best and most comprehensive business information "sources of sources." These list and/or analyze thousands of different sources of business information, and are therefore some of the most important resources in any business library. Because these sources are so all-encompassing, they can often be used as first places to check when undertaking any information search.

American Library Directory
R.R. Bowker
121 Chanlon Road
New Providence, NJ 07974

This is a leading guide to public and academic libraries throughout the United States.

Books in Print
R.R. Bowker
121 Chanlon Road
New Providence, NJ 07974

This is the guide to finding out about published books. Volumes include a title, subject, and author directory, as

well as one that lists names, addresses, and phone numbers for thousands of publishers.

Business Information Sources
Revised Edition, 1985
Lorna M. Daniells
University of California Press
2120 Berkeley Way
Berkeley, CA 94720

This is one of the most well-known business reference guides ever published, and a classic in its field. Daniells is the recently retired head of Harvard

University's Graduate School of Business Administration's Baker Library. *Her book describes and analyzes all of the major business books, reference sources, bibliographies, indices, directories, statistic sources, and more.*

Consultants and Consulting Organizations Directory
Gale Research Company
835 Penobscott Building
Detroit, MI 48226

This is the leading directory of consultants in the United States. It includes geographic as well as major subject indices.

Directories in Print
Gale Research Company
835 Penobscott Building
Detroit, MI 48226

A superb "directory of directories," this book is often an excellent "first stop" when initiating an information search.

Directory of Fee-Based Information Services
Burwell Enterprises
3724 FM 1960 West
Suite 214
Houston, TX 77068

This leading paperbound directory lists all the known "information brokers" and information-gathering services throughout the United

States. *Each entry includes a contact name and number, subject specialties, and other useful information.*

Directory of Special Libraries and Information Centers
Gale Research Company
835 Penobscott Building
Detroit, MI 48226

This is an extensive, authoritative guide to "special" libraries—nontraditional libraries that specialize in particular subjects.

Dow Jones–Irwin Business and Investment Almanac
Dow Jones–Irwin
1818 Ridge Road
Homewood, IL 60430

A comprehensive list of business and financial data, this almanac includes industry surveys, economic indicators, key company data, lists of growth companies, bonds and money-market investment data, and much more. It is an invaluable reference guide.

Encyclopedia of Associations
Gale Research Company
835 Penobscott Building
Detroit, MI 48226

This is an invaluable guide to professional associations throughout the United States, which are typically excellent sources of statistics and expertise. Companion directories are available for state and regional associations, as well as for international associations.

The Encyclopedia of Business Information Sources

Gale Research Company
835 Penobscott Building
Detroit, MI 48226

This directory presents a wide range of business information sources listed under 1,000 alphabetical business subjects. It includes databases, publications, organizations, etc.

Findex: The Directory of Market Research Reports, Studies, and Surveys

Cambridge Information Group
1200 Quince Orchard Boulevard
Gaithersburg, MD 20878

This is a very useful directory listing available market research reports, a full description of each report, and pricing and ordering information.

Find It Fast: How to Uncover Expert Information on Any Subject

HarperCollins
10 East 53rd Street
New York, NY 10022

This volume identifies and describes

various sources of information, analyzes how to perform business research, and advises how to find and interview subject experts for information.

The Fiscal Directory of Fee-Based Information Services in Libraries

FYI/ County of Los
Angeles Public Library
12350 Imperial Highway
Norwalk, CA 90650

This very useful and inexpensive guide lists information services as well as document delivery services for over 200 libraries and information centers throughout the United States.

Gale Directory of Publications

Gale Research Company
835 Penobscott Building
Detroit, MI 48226

A leading guide to finding the names and addresses of thousands of publications and publishers throughout the United States.

The Green Book

New York Chapter
American Marketing
Association
420 Lexington Avenue
New York, NY 10017

This is the leading annual directory of major research firms and research services.

Information Industry Directory
Gale Research Company
835 Penobscott Building
Detroit, MI 48226

This annual guide to 4,000 organizations, publications, and services involved in producing and disseminating electronic information is very useful if you are studying the makeup of the information industry.

Information Sources
Information Industry Association
555 New Jersey Avenue NW
Washington, DC 20001

This directory is published by the leading professional association of major information companies and organizations. It is a "who's who" of those companies, describing what they publish, names of key executives, and other important data.

Lesko's Info-Power
Information USA
10335 Kensington Parkway
Kensington, MD 20895

Written by nationally known expert Matthew Lesko, "Info-Power" is chock-full of names, addresses, phone numbers, and contacts for locating experts within the Federal Government and other official bodies.

Monthly Catalog of United States Government Publications
Superintendent of Documents
Government Printing Office
Washington, DC 20402

One of the standard references for keeping up with what the United States government is publishing, this volume is arranged alphabetically and has an index.

Oxbridge Directory of Newsletters
Oxbridge Communications
150 Fifth Avenue
New York, NY 10011

This is a leading directory for finding names and contact information for the tens of thousands of specialized newsletters published throughout the United States.

Research Centers Directory
Gale Research Company
835 Penobscott Building
Detroit, MI 48226

This is a fascinating directory that lists and describes organizations that conduct research on thousands of different topics.

Standard Periodical Directory
Oxbridge Communications
150 Fifth Avenue
Suite 236
New York, NY 10011

This is another leading directory of magazines and periodicals published throughout the United States.

Subject Collections
R.R. Bowker
121 Chanlon Road
New Providence, NJ 07974

Organized by subject, this is a guide to special collections of university, college, public, and special libraries in the United States.

Ulrich's International Periodicals Directory
R.R. Bowker
121 Chanlon Road
New Providence, NJ 07974

This is an extensive guide to 130,000

periodicals published throughout the world.

United States Government Manual
Superintendent of Documents
Government Printing Office
Washington, DC 20402

This is the official guide to the organization, services, and resources of all of the departments, agencies, and quasi-governmental entities in the United States. It is an excellent manual for understanding how the government is set up, and where to go for information.

Washington Information Directory
Congressional Quarterly
1414 22nd Street NW
Washington, DC 20037

This excellent guide to information resources located in Washington, DC, includes both public and private sources.

Appendix II
Directories of Databases and Database Hosts

ONLINE DATABASE DIRECTORIES

The following is a list of major guides to currently available databases and database vendors.

Computer-Readable Databases
Gale Research Company
835 Penobscott Building
Detroit, MI 48226

A very easy to use, comprehensive directory of computer databases. It includes an introductory article on the state of the database industry, with useful industry statistics.

Datapro Directory of Online Services
Datapro Research Corporation
Delran, NJ 08075

This is a two-volume, loose-leaf directory that lists facts on the online industry and provides buying advice.

Directory of Online Databases
Gale Research Company
835 Penobscott Building
Detroit, MI 48226

This is another excellent guide to databases, published by Gale, the leading reference book publisher.

Directory of Online InformationResources
Capital Systems Group, Inc.
Suite 208
7910 Woodmont Avenue
Bethesda, MD 20814

This directory lists 600 databases.

How to Look It Up Online
St. Martin's Press
175 Fifth Avenue
New York, NY 10010

While not really a database directory, "How to Look It Up Online" is an excellent source book for learning about what types of databases exist and how to perform a search. Author Alfred Glossbrenner is one of the leading "gurus" of teaching online searching, and his book offers an informative and fun way to learn how to get started.

CD–ROM DIRECTORIES

The following is a list of major guides to currently available CD-ROM databases.

The CD-ROM Directory
TFPL
22 Peter's Lane
London, UK EC1M 6DS

This directory lists over 1,500 CD-ROM titles from around the world.

CD-ROMS in Print
Meckler Corporation
11 Ferry Lane West
Westport, CT 06880

This annual directory lists CD-ROM (optical disc) databases.

Directory of Portable Databases
Gale Research Company
835 Penobscott Building
Detroit, MI 48226

This directory includes listings on CD-ROMs as well as other "portable" databases, such as those available on diskettes or tape.

Optical Information Systems
Meckler Corporation
11 Ferry Lane West
Westport, CT 06880

This is another directory of CD-ROM databases.

MAJOR ONLINE DATABASE HOSTS

The following is a list of major online vendors of interest to business. This is not an all-inclusive list by any means, but it does identify those vendors most prominent in the industry.

ADP Network Services, Inc.
175 Jackson Plaza
Ann Arbor, MI 48106
(313) 769-6800

ADP specializes in a wide range of economic and financial databases, and has the capacity to forecast and model the data.

America Online
8619 Westwood Center Drive
Vienna, VA 22182
(800) 827-6364

*America Online is a new, fast grow-
ing service with a wide variety of
news, entertainment, and investment information, as well as bulletin
boards. It's more consumer- than
business-oriented.*

BRS Information Technology
Maxwell Online
8000 Westpark Drive
McLean, VA 22102
(703) 442-0900
(800) 289-4277

*BRS is one of the major online "hosts,"
providing access to many databases
and covering a wide range of subject
matters.*

CIFAR
Center for International
   Financial Analysis and
   Research
211 College Road East
Princeton, NJ 08540
(609) 520-9333

*"Cifarbase" provides current and
historical financial data for over
7,000 companies; 2,600 of them are
European based.*

CompuServe, Inc.
5000 Arlington Center
   Boulevard
Columbus, OH 43220
(614) 457-8600
(800) 848-8990

*This popular system provides gen-
eral and business articles, brokerage
reports, stock quotes, company data,
electronic bulletin boards, and other
consumer and business information.*

Comshare, Inc.
PO Box 1588
3001 South State Street
Ann Arbor, MI 48106
(313) 994-4800

*Databases on this system deal with
international finance, cost-account-
ing, sales potential of specified geographic areas, and related topics.*

**Control Data Corporation/
   Business Information
   Services**
500 West Putnam Avenue
PO Box 7100
Greenwich, CT 06836
(203) 622-2000

*This host specializes in economic and
financial databases, as well as demographics.*

Data Resources Inc. (DRI)/ McGraw-Hill
Data Products Division
Suite 1060
1750 K Street NW
Washington, DC 20006
(202) 663-7720

DRI specializes in databases covering economics and economic forecasts.

Data-Star
485 Devon Park Drive
Suite 110
Wayne, PA 19087
(800) 221-7754

Data-Star is a European-based host accessible in the United States via telecommunication gateways. Data-Star has a number of unique databases that provide key facts and analyses of European companies and industries.

Dialog Information Services, Inc.
3460 Hillview Avenue
Palo Alto, CA 94304
(415) 858-3785
(800) 334-2564

Dialog is the leading online database host, and currently makes available over 380 databases, covering a very wide subject range. Subjects covered include agriculture, biochemistry, biotechnology, chemicals, company statistics, computer science, defense and aerospace, education, electronics, engineering, energy, environment, finance, government, humanities, international business, labor, market research, materials science, medicine, mergers and acquisitions, news, patents, packaging technology, petroleum, pharmaceuticals, physics, psychology, public affairs, regulations, safety, science and technology, social science, tax and accounting, toxicology, tradenames, and much more!*

Dow Jones
PO Box 300
Princeton, NJ 08543
(609) 520-4000

Dow Jones provides online access to extremely current business and financial news, as well as information on sports and weather. Currently Dow Jones offers about 90 databases on their "Dow Jones News Retrieval" system, including the "Asian Wall Street Journal," "Dow Jones Business and Financial Report," "Platt's Oilgram News," "Wall Street Week," "Zacks Earnings and Estimates," "Securities Week," and many more.

European Community Host Organization (ECHO)
177 Route d'Esch
L-1471
Luxembourg
(352) 488-041

The European Community has created a series of databases, many of which are free, that are designed to provide information and advice on the European Community single market.

Interactive Market Systems, Inc.
11 West 42nd Street
New York, NY 10036
(212) 789-3600

A basic tool for the advertising and marketing industries, this host provides information on forecasting, media mix, reach and frequency, market research, and television and radio ratings.

I.P. Sharp Reuters
2 First Canadian Place
Suite 1900
Toronto, Canada M5X IE3
(416) 364-5361

Reuters offers a variety of financial databases, providing data on bonds, money markets, commodities, and other financial markets.

Mead Data Central
PO Box 933
Dayton, OH 45401
(513) 865-6800
(800) 227-4908

Mead is well known in the online industry as a provider of full-text access to a wide range of both legal information (on its "Lexis" database) and general and business news (on its "Nexis" database).

National Data Corporation
Rapidata Division
Corporate Financial Services Division
Corporate Square
Atlanta, GA 30329
(404) 329-8500

Rapidata's concentration is in the banking and investment information areas.

National Library of Medicine
Medlars Management Section
8600 Rockville Pike
Bethesda, MD 20894
(301) 496-6193
(800) 638-8480

Over 35 databases in the health sciences are available from the National Library of Medicine. Major topics include toxicology, general medicine, cancer, and hospital management.

NewsNet Inc.
945 Haverford Road
Bryn Mawr, PA 19010
(215) 527-8030
(800) 345-1301

NewsNet accesses the full text of hundreds of specialized newsletters in many subject areas. Often, the electronic versions of newsletters are available before the print versions.

Prodigy Services Company
445 Hamilton Avenue
White Plains, NY 10601
(800) 776-3449

A consumer-oriented, easy-to-use service providing everything from games and bulletin boards to news and investment information. Owned by Sears and IBM, this service has over 1.7 million users.

Profile Information
Financial Times
Bracken House
10 Cannon Street
London EC 4P, England

The British-based Profile Information is available in the United States via either DataTimes (Oklahoma City, OK) or Vu/Text (Philadelphia, PA). Profile has strong European coverage and a number of databases devoted specifically to the European single market.

Telmar Group
902 Broadway
New York, NY 10010
(212) 460-9000

Telmar supports research efforts for advertising and marketing by offering such databases as "SMRB" ("Simmons Market Research Bureau"), "Arbitron," "Nielsen," "PMB," and others.

Vu/Text
325 Chestnut Street
Philadelphia, PA 19106
(800) 258-8080

Vu/Text, acquired recently by Knight Ridder (which also owns Dialog), specializes in providing regional newspapers from around the country.

Appendix III
Information-Gathering Companies

The following is a list of some of the leading information-gathering services. This list is not all-inclusive by any means, and is restricted to large commercial organizations. Most of these firms offer more than one of the following services: information gathering, consulting, competitive intelligence, custom market research, computer database searching, and document retrieval.

Dynamic Information
1722 Gilbreth Road
PO Box 990
Redwood City, CA 94064

Federal Document Retrieval
810 1st Street, NE
Seventh Floor
Washington, DC 20002

FIND/SVP
625 Avenue of the Americas
New York, NY 10011-2002

Fuld & Company
80 Trowbridge Street
Cambridge, MA 02138

Information on Demand
8000 Westpark Drive
McLean, VA 22102

Information Store
500 Sansome Street
Berkeley, CA 94111

Kirk Tyson International
2021 Midwest Road
Oak Brook, IL 60521

Michael M. Kaiser and Associates
Suite 206
1611 North Kent Street
Arlington, VA 22209

Research on Demand   *Washington Researchers*
2030 Addison Street   2612 P Street, NW
Berkeley, CA 94704   Washington, DC 20007

Teltech Resource
  Network Corporation
2850 Metro Drive
Minneapolis, MN 55425

In addition to the above services, a number of academic and public libraries have established divisions that offer computer database searching and/or certain information retrieval services to the public for a fee. An excellent directory of these services is *The Fiscal Directory of Fee-Based Information Services in Libraries*, published by FYI at the Los Angeles Public Library in Norwalk, California (see Appendix I).

Appendix IV
How-To
Books and Guides

The following is a brief list of books that explain how to perform marketing and other forms of research. Some are standard texts, others are more specialized.

MARKET RESEARCH TEXTS

Cheap But Good Marketing Research
Alan Andreasen
Business One Irwin, 1988

Do It Yourself Marketing Research
George Breen and A.B. Blankenship
McGraw-Hill, 1991

Low-Cost Market Research: A Guide for Small Businesses
Keith Gorton and Isabel Carr
John Wiley and Sons, 1983

Marketing on a Shoestring: Low-Cost Tips for Marketing Your Products or Services
Jeffrey P. Davidson
John Wiley and Sons, 1988

Marketing Research
David J. Luck, Hugh G. Wales, and Donald Taylor, Editors.
Prentice Hall, 1987

The Marketing Sourcebook for Small Businesses
John Wiley and Sons, 1989

State of the Art Marketing
A.B. Blankenship and George Breen
American Marketing Association, 1993

COMPETITIVE INTELLIGENCE BOOKS AND GUIDES

Advances in Competitive Intelligence
John E. Prescott
University of Pittsburgh Press, 1989

Analyzing Your Competition
FIND/SVP, 1991

*The Business Intelligence
   System*
Benjamin and Tamar Gilad
AMACOM Publications, 1988

*Competitor Intelligence: How to
   Get It; How to Use It*
Leonard M. Fuld
John Wiley and Sons, 1985

*Competitor Intelligence Manual
   and Guide*
Kirk Tyson
Kirk Tyson, 1990

*How to Check Out Your
   Competition*
John M. Kelly
John Wiley and Sons, 1987

*How to Find Information About
   Companies*
Lorna M. Daniells, et al
Washington Researchers, 1991

Monitoring the Competition
Leonard M. Fuld
John Wiley and Sons, 1988

Outsmarting the Competition
John J. McGonagle, Jr., and
   Carolyn M. Vella
Sourcebooks Trade, 1990

Appendix V
Guides to Organizing an Information-Gathering System

If you want to establish a library or information center, here are some helpful sources:

The Best of OPL: Five Years of the One-Person Library (1990)
Special Libraries Association
1700 18th Street NW
Washington DC 20009
(202) 234-4700

This is an anthology of articles published in "OPL," a publication written for one-person libraries. Among the subjects covered are marketing and management strategies, as well as a complete bibliography.

Managing Small Special Libraries (1988)
Special Libraries Association
1700 18th Street NW
Washington, DC 20009
(202) 234-4700

This spiral-bound publication focuses on the operation of small libraries, and covers areas such as automation, human resources, management, operations, and so forth. The guide is composed of articles compiled from "Special Libraries" magazine.

Marketing the Modern Information Center (1987)
FIND/SVP
625 Avenue of the Americas
New York, NY 10011
(212) 645-4500

This professional advancement guidebook analyzes the demand and competition for corporate information services delivered from

both within and outside corpora-
tions.It covers internal pricing of
information services, how to en-
hance their value, and other related topics.

**Special Libraries: A Guide
  for Management (1986)**
Special Libraries
  Association
1700 18th Street NW
Washington, DC 20009
(202) 234-4700

*This eighty-five-page guide outlines
how to establish a special library. It
covers topics ranging from use of
computer technology to establishing
resources, and much more.*

American Library Association
50 East Huron Street
Chicago, IL 60611
(312) 944-6780

*This association can be of assistance
in establishing a library. ALA also
publishes a book called "Managing
Small Library Collections in Business and Community Organizations" (1989).*

**American Society for
  Information Science**
Suite 501
8720 Georgia Avenue
Silver Spring, MD 20910-3602
(301) 495-0900

*This is another helpful association in
the field of information science.*

Two other professional associations that may be helpful are
the Information Industry Association, located in Washington,
DC (202-639-8260), and the Society of Competitive Intelligence
Professionals in Washington, DC (202-223-5885).

Appendix VI
A Generalist's Source List

This might seem crazy to any information specialist worth his or her salt, but in this appendix we're going to try to give you a brief list of sources and services that should be familiar to every business generalist.

Our generalist's source list begins with all the previous appendices. It continues with the following annotated list of items and organizations that should be found in any business library, and that every executive should be familiar with.

The Census Catalog and Guide, published by the Bureau of the Census and available from the United States Government Printing Office, is a must, containing a descriptive list of all products and services available from the Census. Don't forget to subscribe to two other essential United States government publications: *County Business Patterns* and *Survey of Current Business*. The former lists employment and payroll statistics, broken down by county, while the latter provides broader aggregate estimates and analyses of United States economic activity as a whole.

The American Statistics Index, published by the Congressional Information Service, is a comprehensive guide to the statistical publications of the United States government.

If you really want to keep up with who the real experts are behind these Federal Government sources, you should probably buy a copy of *Who Knows: A Guide to Washington Experts*, a paperback directory published by Washington Researchers that identifies and provides contact information for thousands of experts in Washington.

For recent financial statements and other information on publicly held companies, everyone should have either or both *Moody's Manuals* (Moody's Investors Services) and *Standard & Poor's Register of Corporations, Directors, and Executives* (Standard and Poor's).

For general information on various industries, there are *Standard & Poor's Industry Surveys* and the annual *United States Industrial Outlook*, published by the United States Department of Commerce.

To discover a company's divisions and subsidiaries, you should have access to *America's Corporate Families*, published by Dun's Marketing Services; it lists 9,000 parent companies worth over $500,000 and their 45,000 subsidiaries and divisions.

Another excellent Dun's directory, this one for finding facts on overseas firms, is *Principal International Businesses*. It lists key facts for over 50,000 firms in 113 countries.

Other guides to international business you should be familiar with include *How to Find Information About Foreign Firms*, published by Washington Researchers, and the series of marketing directories published by the London-based EuroMonitor. You can keep up with what the European Community is publishing by getting a catalog from an organization in Lanham, Maryland, called UNIPUB.

The *Survey of Buying Power* and the *Survey of Industrial Purchasing Power* are two special issues of *Sales and Marketing Management* magazine that should be on every marketing person's shelf. Another key directory covering the marketing field is the *International Directory of Market Research Houses and Services*, published by the American Marketing Association.

Basic international data can be found in the United Nation's *Statistical Yearbook* and *Demographic Yearbook*. No one can do without the *Dun & Bradstreet Million Dollar Directory*, which provides basic information on 160,000 companies. To be included, companies must meet one of the following criteria: net worth of over $500,000, 250 or more employees, or sales of over $25 million. Another key company directory is the *Standard and Poor's Register of Corporations, Directors, and Executives*, which includes information on nearly 40,000 companies.

Finally, a newer and less expensive company directory you may want to check out is *Hoover's Handbook* (Emeryville, CA). This handbook (there are separate United States and world directories) covers only the very largest companies, and is much less comprehensive than the other directories. However, it does provide more details on those firms it does cover, and is a significantly less expensive purchase.

Dun's Business Rankings, Ward's Business Directory, and directories produced by American Business Information list companies according to their Standard Industrial Classification (SIC) codes and sales. Private as well as public companies are included.

The *Standard Directory of Advertisers*, and its companion, the *Directory of Advertising Agencies*, published by the National Register Publishing Company, contain thousands of names of key executives at companies that advertise, as well as their agencies.

The *Thomas Register of American Manufacturers* and the *Thomas Register Catalog File* (Thomas Publishing Company) is a multi-volume set that lists virtually all United States manufacturers of any significance, alphabetically and by product, and also contains reproductions of product catalogs.

The *Dun & Bradstreet Reference Book* is probably the most complete published list of companies and includes their principal SIC number and estimated financial strength rating.

Business Publication Rates and Data, published by the Standard Rate and Data Service, contains a wealth of information on all business publications. Standard Rate and Data also publishes similar directories covering consumer publications, other media, and direct mail lists. The entire set should be in every business library. *Who's Who in America* is published by Marquis Who's Who, which also has companion directories (e.g., *Who's Who in the East, Who's Who of American Women*, etc.).

State Industrial Directories, which describe business and economic activity within particular states, are available from various sources, including State Economic Development offices, chambers of commerce, and private publishers such as American Business Information.

The *Statistical Abstract of the United States*, published by the United States Bureau of the Census, is an information "bible" that includes a wealth of industrial, social, political, and economic statistics, as is the *Information Please Almanac*, published annually by Houghton Mifflin.

No one should forget these two reference basics: the new *Encyclopedia Britannica* and Webster's *Third New International Dictionary of the English Language*.

The index to articles in business periodicals is the *Business Periodicals Index*, published by H.W. Wilson. The published index to articles in general and non-technical publications is the *Reader's Guide to Periodical Literature*, also published by H.W. Wilson.

The index to current information on companies and industries is the *F&S Index of Corporations and Industries*, produced by Predicasts, Inc. In fact, Predicasts has so many other important information services and products that you should request its brochures for your files immediately.

Although the above-mentioned indices are the leading ones in the field, remember that today you can also obtain indices of business literature on CD-ROM, which makes for faster and more efficient searching. A leading provider of business information on CD-ROM is the Information Access Company, 362 Lakeside Drive, Foster City, CA 94404, (415) 378-5000.

Statistics Sources (Gale Research Company) is a good subject guide to data on industrial, business, social, educational, financial, and other topics.

Newsletters in Print, also published by Gale, provides a list of newsletters in thousands of subject fields.

While you're at it, get a list of all the directories and publications of Gale Research, as they are probably the leading business reference publisher in the country, and have a variety of very useful books and publications.

In case this isn't already obvious, every business should subscribe to *Business Week, Forbes, Fortune,* and the *Harvard Business Review* as well as *The New York Times* and *The Wall Street Journal.* Beyond that, your own specific field will determine which periodicals you should read regularly. Smaller companies should subscribe to *Inc.* Executives anxious to keep up should read *Boardroom Reports.* And every business should make sure it receives the leading trade journals in its field. To find out what these are, check the *Gale Directory of Publications* or one of the other periodical directories.

About the Authors

Andrew P. Garvin is president of FIND/SVP, Inc., a leading New York-based consulting, research, and information-gathering service.

Cofounded by Mr. Garvin in 1969, FIND/SVP is part of the worldwide network of SVP consulting and information services. FIND/SVP pioneered the concept of providing information and consulting services by telephone in the United States, and now serves the information and research needs of over 1,700 organizations. It also publishes and distributes a variety of market reports, newsletters, and information products. In 1974, FIND/SVP's Quick Information Service won the Information Industry Association's Product-of-the Year Award.

From 1979 to 1982, Mr. Garvin was a member of the board of directors of the Information Industry Association and was chairman of the 1979 National Information Conference and Exposition. He remains active in the association. Since 1987, he has been a member of the Young Presidents' Organization.

Prior to starting FIND/SVP, Mr. Garvin was vice president of his own public relations and marketing firm, and earlier was a correspondent for *Newsweek*.

A frequent speaker on information-related topics, Mr. Garvin holds a BA in political science from Yale University and an MS in journalism from the Columbia School of Journalism. He lives in New York City with his wife and daughter.

Robert Berkman has spent over ten years in the information business. After graduating from the University of Virginia in 1980, he joined McGraw-Hill Publishing in New York City and worked as a senior editor until 1986. In 1987 he wrote *Find It Fast: How to Uncover Expert Information on Any Subject*, which was published by HarperCollins and revised in 1990. Mr. Berkman is also founder and publisher of *The Information Advisor*, a monthly newsletter for business researchers. He currently lives in Rochester, New York, with his wife and stepdaughter.

Hubert Bermont completed his undergraduate and graduate studies at New York University. He is the executive director of American Consultants League, a senior member of the faculty of the Consultants Institute, and the former publisher of the Consultants Library. Mr. Bermont has written eighteen books.

Index